When You Fast

Barbara Y. Tuggle

ROYSTON
Publishing

BK Royston Publishing
P. O. Box 4321
Jeffersonville, IN 47131
502-802-5385
http://www.bkroystonpublishing.com
bkroystonpublishing@gmail.com

© Copyright – 2017

All Rights Reserved. No part of this book may be reproduced, stored in a retrieval system, or transmitted by any means without the written permission of the author.

Cover Design: Kamaal Designs
Cover Image Credit: JC Penney Portraits

ISBN: 978-1-946111-47-0

Printed in the United States of America

Dedication

I dedicate this book to my two sisters, Brenda and Jackie. When God handed out sisters, I hit the jackpot. All my love to both of you,

Your Big Sister
Barbara

Acknowledgements

I am so thankful for all the help I received in writing this book, and I want to acknowledge a few people who supported me. I love and appreciate each of you very much.

Thanks to my cousins Shunzetta, Anthony, and his wife Duana for your encouragement, assistance, and advice to help me through some tough struggles while working on this project.

Thanks to ALL my girlfriends for having my back in every area of my life, and especially when I was trippin' about this book! Your friendships are valuable to me.

I am particularly grateful for the assistance given by Aunt Betty--you are my biggest supporter. When I had no idea about issues concerning the book, we talked about it and soon I was back on track. Uncle Charles, you got me into this and I am glad you did. If you had not followed the leading of the Holy Spirit to tell me to fast, I would not have written this book. Aunt Shirley, your wisdom is a blessing.

I wish to acknowledge the typing assistance provided by Artricia, Terri, Stuart, and my daughter, Tamira. I could not have gotten the draft to my editor without all of you.

To my pastor, Daniel Shull, thank you for the very valuable insight on fasting "things" as well as food. This made me look for the answer when I thought I had all the answers. You were right, and I am thankful that you were.

I would also like to express my appreciation to Robert for financial assistance. I will always be there for you.

I offer special thanks to my two grandbabies, Nyla and Ariana, for helping me read and research scriptures on fasting. My hope is that you apply what you learned to your life now and in the future.

To my brother, I didn't realize you were going through something at the time our Dad passed. But through it all, you have shown me how much you do care, and I look forward to our getting to know each other better.

SPECIAL THANKS

My deepest thanks are to You, God. I am so grateful You picked me to share Your message with the world about fasting. Every time I needed something or someone, You have provided. You showed me my destiny and future. With Your help, I am pleased to do it. No more backtalk! "Really."

I also thank You, God, for sending me my editor, B. Francheska White from Secretariat Associates, LLC. Francheska, I know God hooked us up and I am so glad He did! You helped me bring my words to life. You shaped and molded my thoughts and words so my passion for fasting could be heard. I would have never completed this assignment without you.

Table of Contents

DEDICATIONS	iii
ACKNOWLEDGEMENTS	iv
INTRODUCTION	xi
THE AGREEMENT—Commitment to a Christian Fast	
PART ONE – FASTING—	1
A SPIRITUAL TOOL— F.A.S.T.	
WHAT'S THE POINT OF FASTING?	
SOMEONE IN YOUR CORNER	
DIFFERENT TYPES OF FASTS	
PART TWO – INTIMACY WITH GOD	55
PRAYER CHANGES THINGS	
FROM BURDENED TO BLESSED	
THE FULL ARMOUR OF GOD	
PART THREE – LET'S DO IT!	101
WHAT TO EXPECT WHEN YOU FAST	
LEADING BY EXAMPLE	
IT'S YOUR TURN TO FAST	
BREAKING THE FAST	
PART FOUR – FEED SOMEONE ELSE	173
TRAIN UP THE CHILD	
FEED MY SHEEP	
FINAL THOUGHTS	195
THINK ABOUT IT!	

PLANNING YOUR FAST

MISCELLANEOUS BLANK FORMS

NOTE: People who have eating disorders, children under 12 years old, and pregnant or nursing mothers should not fast food, unless the foods are snacks or high in sugar.

INTRODUCTION

Food and I are not in a love affair; however, I do have my favorites. I'm a southern girl brought up on homemade collard greens, buttery caramelized candied yams, rich creamy mellow macaroni and cheese. Add to that, hot cornbread baked in a black cast-iron skillet and crispy golden fried chicken! Whew! What a meal! Wait a minute...let's not forget topping all that off with one of my favorite desserts, pecan pie! Now that you have all those images in your head and you're drooling while remembering the smells coming from those tasty foods, let's talk about fasting. That's right! I have the nerve to tell you about fasting, which is not eating any of this! It also includes doing without other things you enjoy. Although I do not love food like billions of people around the world, I do want it to be lip-smacking good. Whether a snack or a meal, I like to eat. As with most people, for years I ate to the point of over indulging. I also ate when I was not hungry. I realize there are people who eat while in stressful situations. That's not me. Because I have always been a very active person in spite of eating rich southern food, I do not have a weight problem. Now you may wonder why I started to fast.

In the summer of 2015, I found myself dealing with family issues that were causing me a lot of stress. I felt lost and helpless to change things, so I talked to my uncle who is a pastor. He told me to fast and pray about it. I have to be honest. I was looking for a quicker solution. My experience with fasting involved a lot of struggling. I knew at that point; maybe, I didn't do things right in the past—my bad. So, I began to research the subject of fasting. I found out there are many kinds of fasts and so many reasons to fast, that a person could spend weeks looking at all of them. One of the most recognizable fasts for me is spiritual fasting; also known as, Christian fasting, which is the type of fasting I do.

Different religions practice fasting and I found one quite fascinating which I will tell you about later.

All periods of fasting have two things in common: giving up eating for a while and struggling through it. I spent hours in bookstores, libraries and searching websites to learn as much as I could understand about fasting. Yet, I was not satisfied. I understood the purpose, types, lengths and great recipes while on a fast. It was all good information. But... no one told me how to get through the struggle of denying myself food while fasting, and what *they* got out of it. I mean, really!

During one of my frequent visits to the bookstore, I stood in the aisle frustrated again. This time I heard God say to me, "The book you are looking for is not there, because you have not written it." That was the first time God asked me to do something, and I was not paying any attention to

Him. Crazy—right? Instead, I just ignored His voice and bought a book written by a well-known pastor of a mega church. In the book, the pastor told me what fasting was and how to pray. It was not on a personal level. I needed to know what to expect on a fast. I found out more about the pastor's church and members, than I did about what to expect. I found out about his walk with God, but what about the struggle when I'm hungry! How do I keep from giving in to temptation and eat anyway? Then I heard God say again, "You write about it." Now you may be thinking, I got right on the task of writing this book. No. I did not—at least not right away. In fact, writing this book was something I struggled with that also led me to a fast. After some time, many conversations and excuses, I surrendered to God. I committed to writing this book about what you go through when you fast to help people work through challenges. Through fasting, a rewarding, miraculous life-changing outcome is available to you. Then, you can share your experiences with someone. This book is my personal testimony taken from a journal I kept while fasting. It tells how to deal with stress and struggles while "doing without" on your fast. Oh, there is one more thing you need to know. Giving up food and delicious beverages are not the only thing we can fast. Keep reading. We will get to that later in the book.

Struggling during fasting will be present each time you do it, and each of us can still have victories and breakthroughs every time. The key is learning how to push past the problem of struggles and press on to receive the rewards of fasting. Make no mistake; Christian fasting is a personal journey between you and God. The great news is this kind of fasting will bless you in ways you cannot imagine. Just remember, the blessings of the Lord are rich and add no sorrow. Fasting should not be a sorry experience.

Fasting has changed my life, and I believe it can change yours! This book is my testimony. I do not eat the way I use to anymore. Food is no longer a substitute for solving problems, and the best part is how my relationship with God changed. I cannot put that into words, but I will try so you will want to find out for yourselves.

Through my personal fasting journey, I will share steps for you to take that will help you during fasting. I am going to get real, so you can identify with my journey when you take yours. As you read these pages, I will answer many questions and you will find out what to expect when you fast. Join me with an open mind and willing heart to see the advantages Christian fasting brings. Allow yourself to be more productive and intimate with a loving God who wants to communicate with you. You will find closeness with God unlike what you have ever experienced. Not only will you have more self-control when eating, other areas of your life will become disciplined. Where time and energy were wasted, you will see progress. Did you know fasting helps you see your problems clearly and solve them effectively? Trust me, it's worth it. Fasting gives you something else to focus on when you are going through trials and tribulations. There are too many wonderful things in store for you when you fast for me to tell you everything. Fasting is personal to each individual, and the exciting part is discovering who you are and who you are becoming during the process. If I had known the things I am sharing with you about fasting when I started years ago, I would have had outcomes that were more successful. However; God knew He could trust me to be open with you about my struggles, weakness, joys and successes, so you too can have wonderful experiences with Him.

Before we get started, please know that you do not have to take your fasting journey by yourself. Allow me to be your guide and permit me to make a few suggestions. First, please take a moment now to email me at whenyoufast@gmail.com. This will allow me to support you with prayer, and answer any questions while you are reading the book and before you begin your first fast. When it gets tough, I can help. Second; on the next page, there is a **COMMITMENT TO A CHRISTIAN FAST** agreement with my name on it as your witness. YAY! When you sign the agreement, you are committing yourself to learning about fasting and following the steps to have a successful outcome. If you choose to go a step further, I encourage you to make this commitment to God. HE'S GOT YOU!

Let's do this! Get ready for a life-changing experience when you fast.

With all my heart,

Barbara Y. Tuggle

Commitment to a Christian Fast

I make a commitment to:

- Give 100% to the times of fasting so I can receive all the benefits that come from that level of commitment.

- I will study the Bible and pray daily.

- I will keep a journal or write down what I am giving up during the fast and what I will eat to keep me on track.

- I commit to fasting for the duration of the time.

- I state that I will honor this contract with every breath in my body.

Signed by: _____

Witnessed by: _____

Date: _____

When You Fast

Part One

FASTING—A SPIRITUAL TOOL

F.A.S.T.

When You Fast

WHAT'S THE POINT OF FASTING?

Things we don't know how to do are the biggest challenges. Especially if we also do not understand the reason or benefits of the assignment before we start on it. My first experience with fasting began about seven years ago when I was a member of a new church. I was excited about this church, enjoyed the preaching and the members were friendly and kind. One Sunday morning after the sermon, the Pastor announced to the congregation that we would begin a corporate 21-day Daniel fast. I thought, okay, so everybody in here is going on this fast. Really? The ushers passed out the plan for the fast. I glanced at it, folded the paper, and put it in my purse with the intention of reading it when I got home later. After returning home and enjoying my 'southern Sunday dinner,' I began relaxing for the evening and remembered the handout. I took the paper from my purse and began to read it. It explained the 21-Day Daniel Fast is a partial fast based on Daniel 10:2-3. During

Barbara Y. Tuggle

the fasting period, I could only eat certain foods, and I should pray throughout the fasting period. Now those certain foods were fruits and vegetables with water as our beverage for a little over four weeks. At that point, my jaw dropped. Four weeks...NOT! I tossed that paper aside. There was no way I was willing to limit myself to that menu. Where's the meat! They gave that paper to the wrong sistah. I did not try to fast—not for a half-day or whole day. My decision was...no way, no day! I did not understand fasting or what was in it for me, so I was not willing to participate. The saddest part of it all was that I did not try to get an understanding. What a mistake! Proverbs 4:5 says; "Get wisdom, get understanding; do not forget my words or turn away from them." At that time, I definitely ignored what the Pastor said while not recognizing he was teaching what God said. As far as fasting was concerned, I was off to a bad start.

Eventually, I moved my membership to another church. I had grown some and when our Pastor asked the

When You Fast

church to fast, I tried it. I wish I could say my times of fasting went well, but it did not. I knew a little more, but not enough to resist the wrong foods while I was on the fast. In my mind, every time I stopped fasting, I was 'cheating' on God. I felt so bad. For me, it was the same feeling I had when an ex-boyfriend cheated on me. Many of us know that feeling. Well, I imagined God hurt like that when I cheated on a fast because of my lack of discipline. I asked God to forgive me. Unfortunately, for me, it seemed to be a pattern. I would start a fast, and then break the fast.

Although I was consistent in my efforts to stay on the fast, when I broke it, I allowed the devil (our enemy) to condemn me as a failure in God's eyes. What was the point of going on a fast, if I could not stay on it until the end?

The answer lies in why a person begins to fast. Before we continue, think of the reasons you are considering fasting or what influenced your decision to fast and then answer the question on the following page.

Barbara Y. Tuggle

What do you hope to achieve through reading this book on fasting?

When I first began fasting, it was because the pastor told the congregation that was the plan for a certain time. I was trying to be obedient, but I still had no knowledge of how to finish the fast. I never thought of fasting on my own outside of a request to do it corporately. It is not wise to fast because it sounds like a good idea, or because it is someone else's instruction. When I got serious about fasting, it was because a lot of stress was influencing decisions I needed to make, and I was looking for peace and help to solve my problems soon.

Fasting requires knowing that what you are doing is beneficial to you. It is not a social thing. It's personal and between YOU and GOD. There should be no guilt or

When You Fast

feelings of any negative consequence for not completing a fast. God will not punish you. Any feeling of being a disappointment to God comes from the devil. Sure, we all want to be successful and complete whatever we are doing and we get disappointed when we don't. However, we cannot let our disappointment stop us from learning more, or stop our determination to get over it and keep moving so we hear from God. Do not let the devil beat you up about cheating.

It took me a couple of years to learn the benefits of fasting and ways to work through struggles. This is a little of what I now know through personal experience:

- Fasting is one of the ways to show God He is first in your life
- Fasting puts who you are, what you own and what you do in the right order
- Fasting helps mature Christians to follow the life of Christ and do the will of God

Barbara Y. Tuggle

- Fasting makes our wild flesh behave—self control
- Fasting corrects personality flaws
- Fasting is a pathway for deeper intimacy with God
- Fasting keeps our selfish nature in check
- Fasting allows you to see all the wonders God has to give you
- When you fast, you can hear what God is saying to you

My journey to spiritual fasting began with my grandmother, but I did not know it at the time. When I was a child, during the summer months my parents would take my sisters, cousins and me to visit my grandmother in Mississippi. She always talked to me about different things that I didn't understand at the time. I thought she meant to talk to someone else because some of what she said was just too deep. For example, although I was very young, my Grandmother told me I was the one who had to keep the family together. What! I wasn't even ten! I would just look

When You Fast

at her with a blank stare, and I believe she knew I did not get her meaning. Now, I know my grandmother was speaking purpose in my life.

As I got older, I found myself always wanting to have my family over to my house for parties and outings. In 2010, one of my cousin's and I decided to have a family reunion. It was a success and everyone had a lot of fun. Later, my cousin said she did not have time to help me with future reunions. In my heart, I wanted to continue our family gatherings. When I remember some of the conversations I had with my grandmother, she knew holding the family together would not be easy, but I could do it.

For the next few years, I planned the family reunions with the help of one of my aunts. Usually, I start a year earlier planning a theme, colors and different activities for all ages, plus anything else to make the event enjoyable. It was during the summer of 2015 that more family members became involved; so did multiple problems. I was planning

Barbara Y. Tuggle

a reunion at a beautiful park called Cumberland Falls State Resort Park in Corbin, Kentucky. This location was about 180 miles away from our hometown of Louisville, Kentucky. It would take a little over 2 ½ hours to drive there. About 100 interested family and friends were excited about this reunion. As the plans continued, my excitement was greater than theirs was until I discovered nothing was going right. Everybody had their own opinions and suggestions, but they were not backing it up with action. I was the one doing all the work. I felt like my whole family was against me, and I learned they were talking about me behind my back. One cousin told me everything, and I knew this would be the last family reunion I would plan. My heart was hurt. I told an uncle, who is also a Pastor, what was going on. He said, "You need to go to God on a more intimate personal level." His words reminded me of something I learned when I was fasting with a church. Our Pastor told us to go to God on a personal level by fasting and praying. Well, I tried that,

When You Fast

but I never completed them and with my "see-saw fasting attitude," I did not realize it mattered. Truthfully, I did not know how to go to God on a personal level. However, my family had a problem with me, and I had one with them. If fasting was going to help me resolve our issues, I needed to know more about it. Therefore, I went to the library and bookstore to find books. Instead, I got an instruction from God to write a book myself.

When I shared the news with my daughter about writing a book, I thought she would be excited for me. Instead, she criticized me and was not encouraging. Although I knew her negative comments were right, she hurt my feelings and I decided not to write it. My heart was heavier with the disappointing response from my daughter, the family reunion, and the need for more information on fasting. I felt helpless and alone with all of it, as the family reunion became more of a burden.

Barbara Y. Tuggle

One month before the reunion, we did not have t-shirts or much money, and I did not know how I was going to feed people. It did not matter what I planned or who helped, I had to finish what I started. I needed help to do that! I decided to do as my uncle suggested and that was to go on a fast. It was the first one I had done in a while and I began it on Friday, July 31, 2015. I decided to give up eating meat. This time, I was determined to pray, read my Bible, and read a book on fasting while on the fast. It was my weekend to work, and not a good time for me to start a fast. When I'm on the job and it is not too busy, I can watch television. Hmmm..., television with all those food commercials, then I told myself a lot of television is not good and decided not to watch it while fasting. Instead, I would read my Bible and a book. During the fast, I still could not believe God told me, Barbara, to write a book on fasting. After all, my fasting record was not good. Every time I

When You Fast

doubted it, God showed me my lack of faith in myself. That made me more determined to do the fast right.

I was at work one evening reading my Bible when I came across a story in Exodus about Moses. His story was very interesting to me, and I did not know why. As a child, I saw the movie on television, but it is not the same as the story in the Bible. When I read it, Moses was an Exodus hero. God was telling Moses—not asking—to do something he did not think he could do. Moses gave many reasons why he thought God should choose someone else, and his final excuse was the way he talked. Moses also told God he needed someone to help him. God told Moses, who do you think made your mouth. Then He went a little further with Moses in verses 12-14:

> [12] So go. I will be with you when you speak. I will give you the words to say."
>
> [13] But Moses said, "My Lord, I beg you to send someone else, not me."
>
> [14] Then the LORD became angry with Moses and said, "All right! I'll give you someone

Barbara Y. Tuggle

to help you. Aaron the Levite is your brother, isn't he? He is a good speaker. In fact, Aaron is already coming to meet you, and he will be happy to see you. *–Exodus 4:12-14 (ERV)*

There it was, what I read was as though God was talking directly to me. Moses did not get his way, but he did get his help. God sent Aaron to the rescue. He was the good speaking brother. Talk about struggles and challenges, Moses had them! God told me to do something that I did not want to do. I also gave Him many excuses why I could not do it. However, just like God told Moses how to do what He wanted, after reading this story, I was confident He would also tell me. I knew He would give me people to help every time I needed it. If God is asking you to do something and you do not want to, I recommend you read Moses' story in Exodus 3 and 4.

Here is how God moved for me while I was on my fast:

When You Fast

On the first day of the fast, God took care of all the money problems for our reunion. Sometimes God moves fast and in unexpected ways. I was expecting God to work at the end of the fast, but He blessed me the very first day.

On the second day of the fast, my nephew called to ask if he and his girlfriend could go to the family reunion. I was surprised! I did not know I needed him, but God did. I called my cousin to see if her son was still going also, and she told me he was not. That was unfortunate for me because I needed her son to do something with the kids. I planned a military theme and my nephew went to a military college, so it was a perfect fit.

On the third day of the fast, God gave me peace.

At the end of the fast, I knew fasting and prayer worked, I also knew I had to write this book on fasting. Giving up meat and television were hard and a big sacrifice. It was worth it!

Barbara Y. Tuggle

The family reunion was awesome. Although 29 out of 100 people attended, I was okay with it. My nephew and my younger cousins did a good job with the children's activities. They marched in the family reunion hall like little soldiers. One of my sister's had originally said she and her husband would not be attending. Surprisingly, she and my brother-in-law came and played a Bible trivia game which allowed older and younger attendees to play. They had prizes and played music, and it was great. Those who attended the reunion had a blessed, wonderful enjoyable time. We all felt God's presence. Although planning the family reunions are a struggle and a burden at times, I love doing them. With the help and strength God gives to me, I will continue to help plan them and fast in the process because it does work.

I knew I needed more information on fasting. I went online to look for more books, searching many sites and

When You Fast

looking at summaries of nearly a hundred books. It was overwhelming, and I was discouraged again. I said to myself, "I cannot do this. All these people have books on fasting. I cannot do it." Then God told me to read the reviews. I did. The readers felt just like me. Now, you need to know something about me, I always read reviews. Still, I said, "I don't have a way to do what You need me to do. I need money to be able to do it."

I did not know we were supposed to ask God for everything we needed. When we ask God for something (especially help with what He told us to do), we will receive it. God gives us what we need, not always what we want. This time, He answered my prayer, needs and wants. My work supervisor had not let me work overtime for at least ten years. Suddenly, I could get all the overtime I wanted. I was able to get a computer. My daughter gave me an IPAD. Then God also gave me the first two people to help me with my book. They were my daughter and her Aunt Terri, who went on eBay and bought me books on fasting.

God can give us what we need before we are ready to use it. He connects the present with the past events to show us He was working things out when we first asked. I did not know why God drew me to the scripture in Exodus until things starting coming together. The story of Moses and his helper, Aaron, are a reminder that when God says, "Yes you can do it." I know I can. God backs His Word up with this scripture,

> [15] "I am with you, and I will protect you everywhere you go. I will bring you back to this land. I will not leave you until I have done what I have promised."
> —*Genesis 28:15 (ERV)*

God has my back, and He has yours too.

When You Fast

SOMEONE IN YOUR CORNER

I love my family! They are my rock! While going through some of the roughest times in my life, they supported me in more ways than I can count. Without a doubt, I know they will always be by my side as long as I live. To add to that blessing is the wisdom I gain from our conversations. As I shared earlier, my grandmother and I talked often when I was a child. Now I have a few relatives who have given me strong advice and spiritual wisdom. In fact, the uncle who told me to fast and pray for the family reunion is my Uncle Charles. I go to him or my Aunt Shirley, his wife, for answers to questions I do not understand, and they always break it down for me. This reminds me of the scripture about strength in numbers:

> [12] "An enemy might be able to defeat one person, but two people can stand back-to-back to defend each other. And three people are even stronger. They are like a rope that has three parts wrapped together—it is very hard to break."
> — *Ecclesiastes 4:9-12 (ERV)*

Barbara Y. Tuggle

That's right, everybody needs somebody. It is important to have a mentor and or friends who can give you sound wisdom regarding the scriptures, and a confidant to talk about different issues of life. Some of us are fortunate to have all of those character traits in one or two people. The rest of us need a gang of folks. In Biblical times, the Israelites did not realize they had a friend in the prophets. They knew prophets gave messages from God, but all they really wanted to hear was good news. Just keep all the rest of that stuff to yourself! Isn't that like us today; the things that are in our best interest to help us in our walk with Christ are the things we reject. The attitude of always wanting to have it 'our way' has to change and it does when we fast and pray about it. I knew the challenge of writing this book would not be easy, but I still wanted the easy way out.

One day I was having a phone conversation with my Uncle Charles. I told him I was planning to write a book

When You Fast

about fasting. He advised me to read Isaiah 58. Although thousands of years ago, the prophets were not the most popular guys on the block, their message is just as important today. The great news is we have the advantage of hearing what prophets said by reading our Bible. Isaiah was a prophet who taught the Israelites about true fasting.

When I began to read Isaiah 58, I chose the King James Version. After stumbling through the "est" endings on words and the use of "thou" and "thee" spread through the chapter, I was lost and a little confused. That is when I went to Aunt Shirley to help a sistah out and tell me what in the world did all of that meant. Aunt Shirley is an Evangelist, and always willing to teach everyone who asks. I met with her at the home of Terri, who is also my best friend. Terri is one of my close confidants and a great supporter, while I was writing this book. Aunt Shirley set the atmosphere for us to receive God's Word, and then she explained each verse one by one. When she finished, the anointing of God was all over us. We were high on that Word! What Aunt Shirley taught us is just too good to keep to myself. So the message is in italics under each verse of Isaiah 58 from the King James Version. Prepare yourself for a feast before the fast.

> "[1]Cry aloud, spare not, lift up thy voice like a trumpet, and shew my people their transgression, and the house of Jacob their sins."

Through Isaiah the prophet, God is telling the people to cry aloud with open mouths. Do not hold anything back. Yell it out to them loudly like a trumpet. When you cry out to God in whatever you are doing, you are pouring out yourself to him. You are humbling yourself before God. He said to tell Him of their sins. The children of Israel were constantly doing things so they were fasting, but not according to God's will.

> "[2] Yet they seek me daily, and delight to know my ways, as a nation that did righteousness and forsook not the ordinance of their God: they ask of me the ordinances of justice; they take delight in approaching to God."

We may say that we are seeking God daily, but are we really doing it according to His Word.

When You Fast

"³ Wherefore have we fasted, say they, and thou seest not? Wherefore have we afflicted our soul, and thou takest no knowledge? Behold, in the day of your fast ye find pleasure, and exact all your labours."

When we go on a fast, do we even know what fasting is and why we are doing it? Are we truly seeking God to strengthen our relationship with Him? Or are we fasting because we feel like it is the right thing to do because we heard about it so we seek God for our own pleasure? We say we are giving up things for God, but are we really just doing it to see what God will give us? Do we go around trying to look the part of someone who is fasting but still doing what we want to do while on the fast?

"⁴ Behold, ye fast for strife and debate, and to smite with the fist of wickedness: ye shall not fast as ye do this day, to make your voice to be heard on high."

Do we really think just because we say we are fasting that we are getting through to God even though we don't know why we are fasting? Although we know we are still going about our wicked lives, God will still hear us by just saying we are fasting. Is our fast the way God instructed us to or the way we want to fast?

"⁵ Is it such a fast that I have chosen? A day for a man to afflict his soul? Is it to bow down his head as a bulrush, and to spread sackcloth and ashes under him? Wilt thou call this a fast, and an acceptable day to the LORD?"

Do we just want to look like we are fasting? Do we want to follow all the steps and say that we did a good fast? God is saying all of that is no good. It is of no use anymore. You should never start a fast where you have not sought God first and asked Him what is acceptable. You should never go on a fast before praying to God and asking Him to lead you and to prepare your heart and mind. Ask Him for strength and staying power to stick with the fast and not give up.

"⁶ Is not this the fast that I have chosen to loose the bands of wickedness, to undo the heavy burdens, and to let the oppressed go free, and that ye break every yoke?"

Everything we do should be according to God's will. God is telling us this is what fasting is all about. All that sackcloth and ashes stuff (a sign of repentance and at times of prayer for deliverance) is one thing, but what He wants is for us to be free from wickedness and heavy burdens. He wants us to be free from the yokes in our life. The things in our life that have us burdened can be released off of us through fasting and prayer according to God's will.

"⁷ Is it not to deal thy bread to the hungry, and that thou bring the poor that are cast out to thy house? When thou seest the naked, that

When You Fast

thou cover him; and that thou hide not thyself from thine own flesh?"

This does not mean to bring everyone to your house. "To deal thy bread" means to give what you know of the Word to those who don't know it, and those who don't know God for themselves. When you see they are hungry for something, share what you have. Try to bring them along. If you see someone who is still living in sin, especially in an area you know was a weakness for you, don't start talking about him or her as if you overcame on your own. To cover is to protect them until they are able to free themselves through Jesus Christ.

"8 Then shall thy light break forth as the morning, and thine health shall spring forth speedily: and thy righteousness shall go before thee; the glory of the LORD shall be thy reward."

God wants us to know He has got us covered. He wants us to have faith that He can do all things. When we are fasting and praying to God to break a yoke or to heal a sickness, we have to believe He will do it.

"9 Then shalt thou call, and the LORD shall answer; thou shalt cry, and he shall say, Here I am. If thou take away from the midst of thee the yoke, the putting forth of the finger, and speaking vanity;"

Barbara Y. Tuggle

Fasting and praying according to the will of God will set us free. We can call on God whenever and wherever and He will answer our prayers. When we are fasting and praying for God to release us from whatever has been holding us back, don't think we can talk about what is holding someone else back. Don't point fingers and speak wickedness over someone else's life. Pray for them to know God and His freedom.

"10 And if thou draw out thy soul to the hungry, and satisfy the afflicted soul; then shall thy light rise in obscurity, and thy darkness be as the noon day:"

We have to be willing to pour out ourselves to God and to cry aloud for those who haven't learned to cry out for themselves. The strong must bear the infirmities of the weak. When we do, this is according to God's will. He can turn the dark days to light, lift our heavy burdens, and free us from our sins.

"11 And the LORD shall guide thee continually, and satisfy thy soul in drought, and make fat thy bones: and thou shalt be like a watered garden, and like a spring of water, whose waters fail not."

God knows our heart and our minds. When we humble ourselves to Him and pray for help, He will help us. He will always guide us. God will satisfy us and He will be enough to keep us satisfied. God can make us healthy and strong. He will not fail us.

When You Fast

"¹² And they that shall be of thee shall build the old waste places: thou shalt raise up the foundations of many generations; and thou shalt be called, The repairer of the breach, The restorer of paths to dwell in."

God can rebuild us. He can take our brokenness and lift us up out of our sins. He can break the generational curses. God can set us on a new path to freedom from our yokes.

"¹³ If thou turn away thy foot from the Sabbath, from doing thy pleasure on my holy day; and call the Sabbath a delight, the holy of the LORD, honourable; and shalt honour him, not doing thine own ways, nor finding thine own pleasure, nor speaking thine own words:"

Fasting, praying, and seeking pleases God. The Sabbath day is the Lord's Day. We should seek to serve God every day. We are to keep the Sabbath Holy and rejoice and be glad and honor Him. We should try not to be so self-centered and self-focused while only looking to please ourselves, and seeking God for our own needs as we go about the day saying and doing anything. When fasting and praying, we should always be mindful that we are seeking to please God. So, our mind should be on Him. Our thoughts should be about Him, and we should be talking to Him.

"¹⁴ Then shalt thou delight thyself in the LORD; and I will cause thee to ride upon the high places of the earth, and feed thee with the heritage of Jacob thy father: for the mouth of the LORD hath spoken it. (KJV)"

God wants us to want Him. He wants us to have a deep relationship with Him and have faith in what He can do. When we cry out to God through fasting and praying, without focusing on seeking Him for our own pleasure, then He lifts our burdens and releases us from our fears and doubts. God will truly break our yokes.

I realize scriptures mean different things to each of us depending on where we are in our life. For the first time, I completely understood God's view of fasting from these scriptures. I finally got it! Initially, I think my approach to fasting was something that was customary for church people, especially at the beginning of the year. Maybe some of us who did join in, did it out of habit, whether we were successful or not. One of the reasons for my failure is that I had no knowledge.

When You Fast

God knew my heart was pure in wanting to write about fasting, and He knew I needed to understand the importance of it as a spiritual tool for Christians. I thank God for giving me Uncle Charles and Aunt Shirley as mentors and teachers who obeyed His lead to point me to the Word. Reading Isaiah 58 gave me direction and opened my mind and heart to examine my motives for fasting. If we do not fast with a sincere heart of obedience, God is not going to accept our fast. We will not see our changes or anything we ask Him to do for us. So why do it? If it is to lose weight—go for it. However, we should not consider spiritual fasting as a form of dieting. We can ask God to help us not eat so much at one time or too many calories anytime. If you are fasting for a cause, I hope it is to raise money for an organization to help the less fortunate. What I am saying is, if you have no clear direction and no true reason for fasting, then you are wasting your time and probably missing out on a few self-satisfying meals. So go ahead and get your grub on. However, if that is not you, then Isaiah 58 will give the order of fasting. It will get you on track towards a successful outcome.

I found out something else that I never knew: fasting breaks yokes! Aunt Shirley taught me in a part of verse 6, "The things in our life that have us burdened can be released off of us through fasting and praying according to God's will." Those *'things'* are yokes—heavy burdens. All the stuff that lays heavy on our heart slows us down or stop us from moving forward can come off! You don't even know how that piece of information changed me. But you are going to find out when I get more into yokes in Part 2. For now, it is important for you to take a moment and read Isaiah 58 again; it is an eye opener for sure. Think about each verse and choose a few that stand out to you. On the next page, write down how the verses you chose apply to your life.

When You Fast

Barbara Y. Tuggle

Not only does God have your back in every situation, He places the right people in your life to help. We have to pay attention, so we recognize whom God sends. Having Uncle Charles and Aunt Shirley in my life as mentors has blessed me in more ways than I can say. I continue to learn from them each time we talk. Look at your friends and family to find someone who can truly support you when you fast. I mean someone who has done it and made it a part of his or her lifestyle. If you do not know anyone, ask God to send that person into your life. When you first begin fasting, it will be to your advantage to have support from people who can stand with you. I wrote this book with the intention of not only informing readers about what to expect I will also support you during fasting periods. Therefore, feel free to reach out to me.

If you are around people who are not living their life as a Christian, they are usually doing what they want to do

When You Fast

and not God's will. Consequently, you will find maintaining your fast will be difficult. Be careful when you fast that you do not act like you are not converted. During fasting, God expects us to live and act a certain way other than everybody else. You do not want to expose yourself to people who have wild, uncontrollable behaviors. Fasting opens your inner self, and you are weaker. It is very important for you to cover yourself with prayer and stay away from environments and people who are not on your side. Pay close attention to where you go, and whom you are around during times of fasting. A fun-filled family gathering, sports event or other activity may not be the best place for you when you fast.

During my search for information to write this book, I wanted to know more about fasting from the viewpoint of other spiritual leaders. My first contact was the pastor of the church I was attending. Our meeting was brief and did not meet my expectations. After leaving my pastor's office, I was frustrated and confused. My desire was to gain insight into the spiritual side of fasting from someone outside my circle of family and friends. Therefore, I looked for that person the old-fashioned way, which was from the telephone book. One morning while calling churches in my community, I was able to make an appointment with a pastor who would meet with me as soon as I could get to the church. He gave me directions, and I immediately set out for our appointment.

I was excited about the meeting and had many questions. As I was driving through my neighborhood onto the main street, I soon realized the route was familiar. After arriving at the church, surprisingly I recognized it as the one I often passed. The church sign always had the most interesting, encouraging words that caught my attention. It crossed my mind to visit, but I never did. I had not heard of the pastor until picking this church from the phone listing an

When You Fast

hour earlier. Now I was going to meet him. I will refer to him as Brother C. I had no idea this pastor would open my eyes to fasting on another level. Look at what he says in the next section.

When You Fast

DIFFERENT TYPES OF FASTS

Before I get into the different kinds of fasts, let's go a little deeper about what fasting is. We fast to abstain from all or some kind of food or drink especially in religious observances. Webster's Dictionary defines abstaining as: *"to restrain oneself from doing or enjoying something; to hold oneself back voluntarily; do without; refrain."* Fasting brings our flesh into submission, so we do not give in to different temptations. Submission is: *"the state of being obedient; the act of accepting the authority or control over someone or something else."* We cannot change the definition of fasting, but if done for the Lord it is always more than just giving up food. For a long time, I thought fasting food was the only way to fast. As I continued this way of fasting, I had questions about whether it was acceptable to give up other things instead of food. That is where Brother C comes in. His discussion with me changed the way I looked at fasting and shifted my attitude about it.

There is also a correct attitude about fasting that helps us receive what we are seeking. Yes, it's true; fasting begins with having the right attitude.

Meeting with Brother C

As I walked through the front doors of the church, I felt God's presence. It was so peaceful and welcoming inside. I was confident Brother C would give me answers to my questions. To my right, was an office from which a cheerful, attractive and professionally dressed woman came to greet me. She smiled and said Brother C was expecting me. As we exchanged small talk, he came from his office. Brother C was a handsome man with salt and pepper curly hair, neatly trimmed mustache, and gentle blue eyes. He smiled, shook my hand, held it for a moment and with a friendly deep voice he said, "It is a pleasure to meet someone who wants to know about fasting." I followed Brother C into his office, which looked like a small library. I was amazed

When You Fast

and commented on the many books on the shelves. He responded that the only book he will use to discuss fasting with me is the Bible. I sat down in a comfortable chair, and he sat facing me a few feet away. As Brother C began to talk, I found him to be very knowledgeable and confident about what he was saying.

We began our conversation discussing what Jesus taught about the lifestyle of Christians, which we find in the book of Matthew 6. Brother C and I talked for a long time about this teaching, and he explained there are three examples Jesus gave of how we show our Christianity:

In our giving (charitable deeds)

In our praying

In our fasting

Jesus looks at our motives in all these areas. Imagine Him asking these questions to all of us:

Barbara Y. Tuggle

Why are you doing what you are doing?

Why are you giving?

Why are you praying?

Why are you fasting?

How would you answer? When we really think about it, this tells us, there's a right way to 'give' and a wrong way. There's a right way to 'pray' and a wrong way. There's a right way to 'fast' and a wrong way. In these chapters, we find Jesus tells us to be true Christians, help others or charitable organizations, fast, pray and do all of it in secret without boasting to everyone about when and what we are doing.

> "Be careful! When you do something good, don't do it in front of others so that they will see you. If you do that, you will have no reward from your Father in heaven." – Matt 6:1 (ERV)

When You Fast

Jesus said whatever you do in secret, your Father in heaven will see you and reward you openly. Everybody will see how you are blessed, but will not know why.

Our prayer is the same way. People really do not like to put their business in the streets. Therefore, what goes on between you and God is between you and God. Jesus said, "When you fast" do not be like hypocrites with a sad face, because you draw attention to yourself so it will appear like you are fasting. As my grandmother would say, "You're just trying to be seen." or "You're showing off." It is not necessary. When you fast, be yourself, and God will reward you openly. Brother C said when his church has a big decision to make, he will say to the congregation, "This will be a good time for us to fast." In addition, he believes fasting and prayer go together. He does not command the church to do it, because he does not know who can fast and who cannot. It is not important to him to know. He does hope that the church will voluntarily fast along with him and his family. Brother C believes God leaves it up to the individual to fast, because some people physically cannot fast food for medical reasons.

Then, Brother C pointed out the most interesting part of our conversation that really shifted my thinking. He said, Jesus did not specifically say, 'when you fast food or drink.' Personally, I went to the meeting believing that fasting food is important; however, now I understand there is more to it than abstaining from food. Whatever the thing is we give up, it is between God and that person. In Acts 13, there is a good example of the church sending out two missionaries who fasted and prayed before they went on a missionary trip.

So, the question is: 'When you fast, must we always choose to give up foods?' Go to Acts 13 and read the entire chapter. The issue before Barnabas, Simeon, Lucius, Manaen and Saul was: 'Which of them would go on this mission?' Of these five men, they wanted to know which of

When You Fast

them God wanted to send, so as they fasted and prayed to make the right choice. However, we do not know if they fasted 24 hours, 7 days, how long it was, or if it was food. We automatically think it was food, but the scripture does not say.

We think our fast should be from food, because when you mention fasting that's the first thing that comes to our mind. However, we are concluding something that God did not say. He just said Saul and Barnabas fasted. What did they give up? We don't know. It could have been food or it could have been something they chose to do. However, whatever these men fasted, prayer went with it. When we put Acts 13 and Matthew 6 together, we can conclude that it is up to each person.

For the remainder of the day, I thought about my meeting with Brother C and I was satisfied. When I woke up the next morning, I remembered Brother C's answer to my question about where in the Bible does it say we have to fast. Brother C said, "It doesn't." Jesus said, "When you fast," which leads me to believe it is expected of Christians. At that point, I knew I had the title of my book, "When You Fast."

Anything we can temporarily give up to focus on God's will in our life is good for us. We will always get more than we give up. When we spend more time with people and things that take us away from healthy lifestyles, it is time to control our flesh. The Bible gives some examples of fasting to concentrate on spending time with God. In Ezra 10:6, Esther 4:16 and Acts 9:9, they did not eat food or drink water at all in addition to not taking a bath. For myself, I don't know what was up with not bathing, because I would definitely have to stay away from people if I did that for a long period. However, we can also abstain from sex, phones, television, video games, all types of liquor and wine, cigarettes, or anything else that brings pleasure to our flesh. Whatever type of fast you choose to go on, focus on denying

When You Fast

your flesh so your spirit grows and maintains control. That leads to glorifying God. Personally, during different times of fasting, I have given up meat, sweets, bread, dairy and eaten only vegetables and drank juices. I have also given up comforts such as lights in my home, television, phone conversations, social activities, and radio. There is no real formula to determine which type of fast to go on. When you fast, you will hear God clearer than ever, and you will know what to give up and for how long.

Listed below are different kinds of fasts that various people choose to follow.

1. Liquid fast —Refraining from eating all food, but you can drink water and juice. You can make juice from almost any fruit or vegetable and drink it with water, but do not consume food.

2. Partial fast—Refraining from certain types of food (Daniel 10:2-3)

3. Full fast—No food and nothing to drink (Acts 9:9, Esther 4:15-16)

4. Sexual fast–Husband and wife agree to abstain from intercourse. (I Corinthians 7:3-6)

5. Corporate fast—When a person links up with a body of Christian believers for prayer with a specific goal in mind. One person fasting is powerful, but a group of people fasting multiplies power. (I Samuel 7:5-6, Ezra 8:21-23)

6. Absolute fast—Jesus fasted for 40 days (Matthew 4:1 &2)

When You Fast

Muslim Fasting

There are many religions around the world that fast. I found the discipline involved during the Islamic fasting period of Ramadan to be fascinating, because they have a schedule and remain committed to it. Abdul Wakil, a friend of mine is Muslim. He has been practicing for over 16 years and prayer is a part of his daily life. One evening in May, he and I had an insightful discussion about fasting from the Islamic perspective.

He told me Muslims all over the world fast during Ramadan. Muslims say special prayers and some read the entire Qur'an, which they recite in many Masjids (Muslim place of prostrating and worship) during the sacred month. Muslims believe the Qur'an is a divine revelation from Allah (Arabic for God) given over a period of 23 years during the month of Ramadan to and through the prophet Muhammad, his messenger. Ramadan falls at the sighting of the crescent moon indicating the start of each month of the Islamic lunar calendar. During that month, every member of Muslim households should spend it observing the fast unless they are ill or on a journey. Muslims understand that fasting heals the body, heart, and soul, and helps build self-restraint, compassion for the hungry and poor, but most importantly increases god consciousness. They seek to have prayers answered on the night of Decree.

Muslims must abstain from eating and drinking from dawn to dusk. Surah 2 v187 in the Qur'an states that all sexual contact between married couples is also prohibited. It further advises to seek what Allah has made law for them and eat or drink until the white thread (light) of dawn. Then complete their fast until this appears, but to not associate with their wives. They are allowed to break the fast with a sip of water.

Muslims have five daily prayers at specific times. Families will partake in a breaking of fast meal known as 'Iftar,' according to the prophet's teachings. Abdul Wakil

When You Fast

says Allah commands Muslims throughout the world to complete the period of fasting to benefit themselves and glorify him that they may be successful, in accordance with his guidance. Therefore, they should be grateful and obey him.

Our meeting ran late and it was close to Abdul Wakil's prayer time. He needed to determine the direction of The Kaaba, the first place built for worship for mankind by Abraham and his son Ismael. Worldwide, all Muslims turn to offer prayer to Allah in unison signifying unity among the believers.

I didn't want to leave while he was praying. Realizing there were people throughout the world who were praying at the precise hour was so spiritual to me, and I felt the presence of God. I respect the Muslim way of life and their commitment to worshipping and fasting as one. Whether you are Christian, Muslim, or follow the practices of the many other religions who fast, it is interesting to me

Barbara Y. Tuggle

how fasting is a way of drawing closer to one's god; how it is used to show discipline and commitment in one's faith.

Shortly after my conversation with Abdul Wakil, the month of Ramadan was approaching, so I called him to ask if Ramadan had begun. He said it had begun. So I went into my living room, sat on the sofa in front of the window and looked over the tips of my neighbor's tree to get a glimpse of the moon. I did not see it, so I went outside and searched from my porch. I still could not see the moon from my house. It had rained earlier in the day and the air was quite cool. I went back into the house, grabbed a jacket and ran to my car. I was determined to see the moon that night. As I drove down the street a few blocks, while searching the sky and trying to keep my eyes on the street too, I wondered why I could not see it. I turned at the corner, and suddenly there it was. The moon was a bright coral-red color, and the sight of it just took my breath away. A warm feeling poured over me from my head to my toes as I stared at the huge moon.

When You Fast

Slowly I turned the car around to head home. All kinds of thoughts were going through my mind about prayer, the conversations with Abdul Wakil and Brother C, the book; then I looked up ahead to the sky and to my surprise, I saw a rainbow. My mouth dropped open and my body melted into my seat at the sight of that beautiful, multicolored arch seemed to rest over my neighbor's house and mine. I don't know if it was the rainbow, the moon or the fast I was on or just all of it, but my excitement rose up in a loud prayer. The presence of God filled my car and I told Him all about the things concerning neighbors, my family, and me as my prayers poured endlessly from my mouth. I experienced intimacy with God that evening as though we were on a date. It was just He and I loving on each other. God removed my stress and concerns. He left me with such a comforting feeling and assurance that I was on the right track with my book and times of fasting. I knew I could trust Him for everything I needed, and I will forever be grateful for that moment.

When we keep an open mind, we can learn so much from each other regardless of cultural or religious differences. A community pastor taught me not to make assumptions that refraining from eating food was the only way to fast. While a Muslim friend told me how a religion practiced around the world comes together with strong conviction, dedication and <u>one discipline</u> to fast and pray. The conversations I shared with these two men made me want to step up to another level in my Christian life. I sensed a humble spirit from both of them. They believe they are always low-key, never boastful, and quiet about fasting, because they see it as a relationship between them and God, not one for the public eye. I see that in both of them too, and I agree it is between God and us individually.

When You Fast

Earlier in this section, I gave a list of common fasts people choose to follow. I want to add one more to the list: Whatever things take up valuable time and bring your flesh great pleasure, try to fast those things as well for a fulfilling experience of closeness with God.

When You Fast

Part Two

INTIMACY WITH GOD

When You Fast

PRAYER CHANGES THINGS

*Now I lay me down to sleep,
I pray the Lord my soul to keep.
If I should die before I wake,
I pray the Lord my soul to take. Amen*

Leticia is a friend I have known since we were about 8 years old. One day we were talking, and she told me her Mom taught her this prayer when she was old enough to talk. It was simple and to the point, and she repeated it after her Mom until she could say it by herself. Each night throughout her childhood, she would kneel beside her bed and say that prayer. Leticia taught this prayer to her children, and they continue to pass it on as well. My grandmother taught me how to pray when I was 10. It was so special then. I believed God heard me, and I felt close to Him. But, it has not always been this way with God and me. As I got older, I did not say prayers as often. I was smarter, curious and a lot bolder which led me to do things wrong at times that had serious consequences. After forming my own ideas, decisions and personality, I was living my life the way I wanted. We have all been there. Sometimes I was happy and sometimes I was not, but it was my life. I did not talk to God daily. In fact, while I was living my life 'my way,' I prayed for what I needed, wanted, when in trouble or sick, and each time it was brief. They were "help me" or "get me out of this" types of prayers. I don't think my requests left the place where I prayed them; and when God did answer, it was because of His mercy towards me.

Everybody knows people are not perfect; that is except, for a few people who think they are a step below being perfect. The problem is we can see failures and limits in others, but not in ourselves. Deep in our hearts, we know where we miss it and most of our weaknesses. We just don't want to admit it or have someone else tell us about our weaknesses. There are also times when we think we are great to be around, and people should be happy to see us coming. Really? Maybe some people are putting up with

When You Fast

our mess, while others are praying we will change or avoiding us by staying away.

Not only did God speak to the Israelites through prophets, He also talked directly to a few people, like Jesus, Adam, Eve, Ezekiel, Moses and Elijah. Today, I know God speaks through people to get a message to me, and He speaks directly to me. If I hear something from some else that God already said, it's because I didn't move on it when He told me. God confirms His Word with scripture or through something or someone else. This I know for sure. God talks to me, because that's the kind of relationship we have. Now when I pray, it is to get God's direction for my life and an understanding of where He is leading me. I pray because I love Him. One morning as I was praying, I heard the Spirit of the Lord say, "Wait, I have something to tell you." I admit it was usually a one-sided conversation, but this time I stopped and listened. From that point, I seldom begin to get deep into prayer in the morning. Instead, I meditate and wait to hear God speak to me, and then I began to pray.

After understanding fasting better, shifting my attitude and a lot of time spent listening to God the first time, I know we have a relationship. I am more accepting of what God tells me. I am confident that God is caring, tender and affectionate because everything about me is important to Him. God shows His love to me; and because of our intimate relationship, I try to show it too. The best part of all of this is that we keep getting closer as I spend time with Him, and that is because prayer changes things.

Think of the closeness you have with the opposite sex, friends, family, neighbors or whomever. It is not just about saying, "I love you" that makes the relationship tight. From your heart, you must give time and energy to a relationship regularly. You have to open your heart to trust the other person. When you do, just thinking of that person brings a smile to your face. If you smell a scent, it reminds

When You Fast

you of someone special to you. Somehow, you feel each touch you exchanged when you are apart. Now take those feelings, multiply them thousands of times over, and apply them to intimacy with God. That is as close as I can describe it. You see, it is personal. I trust God with all that I am, and my love for Him is real. I know without any doubt that He loves me. I feel His touch everywhere. When the wind blows over my body or the sun warms my face and especially while looking at clouds or a moonlit night, I feel God's presence for real!

Intimacy with God comes through prayer, and we carry it with us always, which is part of our spiritual growth. Together fasting and prayer, give God an opportunity to move in our heart. He will show us things our flesh is holding on to which affects our relationship with Him. You can bet that if God has a problem with your personality, other people do too. Once God reveals our ugly side, we will want to change. When God shows you who you are, trust me, it is not pretty! Consequently, fasting is necessary to flush out poison inside us that is physical and spiritual. It sharpens and improves our sight, hearing, taste, touch, and smell. When you fast and pray, faith grows, and you will realize things you thought were not possible will become possible. Before beginning a fast, it is good to acknowledge Jesus as our Lord, repent of all sins and ask God to forgive us.

> "[9] If you openly say, "Jesus is Lord" and believe in your heart that God raised him from death, you will be saved. [10] Yes, we believe in Jesus deep in our hearts, and so we are made right with God. And we openly say that we believe in him, and so we are saved."
> –Rom. 10:9-10 (ERV)

A prayer of repentance shows we are sorry for things we did wrong and that we want to do what is right.

On the following page, are a few scriptures about praying and fasting. Read each one. In the boxes next to the scripture, write the name(s) of all those who are fasting and the reason for the fast.

When You Fast

Scripture Reference	Who is Fasting	Reason for the Fast
Luke 2:36-38		
Luke 5:33		
Acts 13:3		
Acts 14:21-23		
Nehemiah 1:3-4		
Ezra 8:21-23		

Of all the things prayer changes, it changes us the most. God may not move as quickly as we desire or give us everything we want the way we want it. All of us have experienced that. But, prayer with fasting will affect how we see God, show us how He sees us, and affect our overall behavior. When we include regular fasting in our lives, stresses, anxiety, and issues of life will not weigh on us and become yokes. We will clearly see those things as burdens because God will reveal them through prayer and help us to resolve it.

When You Fast

FROM BURDENED TO BLESSED

What is a Yoke?

The dictionary defines a yoke as: 'a wooden crosspiece fastened over the necks of two animals and attached to the plow or cart that the animal will pull.'

Matthew 11:28 says,

> "Come to me all of you who are tired from the heavy burden you have been forced to carry. I will give you rest. ²⁹ Accept my teaching. Learn from me. I am gentle and humble in spirit. And you will be able to get some rest. ³⁰ Yes, the teaching that I ask you to accept is easy. The load I give you to carry is light."

In Part 1, the basis of true fasting was explained in Isaiah 58. Verses 3-5 speak about yokes:

Barbara Y. Tuggle

"You need to do more in your everyday life. Fasting is just the beginning. You have things that have a hold on you. You need to break every yoke." **(Isaiah 58:3- 5) ERV**

From this verse, we see a yoke can be anything. For example, a bad habit, an addiction you cannot break or even people. Whatever it is, if it is holding you back, it is a yoke, and we all had or still have one or more. We know about some of them, maybe ignore a few or don't know about the others we have or who it is holding us. Whether we put a heavy burden on ourselves or someone forces us to carry it, one thing is for sure, we need to break every yoke. If you try to break a bad habit but have no success, ask God to help you identify the core of the bad habit and/or addiction. However, to hear God clearly, you will need to fast. Before you begin to fast, identify it by giving it a name. When you name the bad habit and/or addiction, this is your first step to breaking it because you acknowledge it is there. You can also think of a yoke as a symbol of slavery because it is

When You Fast

anything that is imposed on us (whether we want it or not). Therefore, whatever or whoever is imposing the yoke also controls us resulting in our serving them or it in any kind of way. Oh yes, you have a yoke or two—everybody does at some point in life. I don't want to make an assumption. So if you don't have any yokes, that's great. Maybe you can help someone else who has a yoke.

Now I am going to let you in on something, I discovered there were two things in my life yoking me that became messy and distracting. The very good news is that both yokes were broken through fasting and prayer. Before I will tell you how to break a yoke, I am going to share my personal story including the good, bad and ugly of these yokes. I won't hold anything back from you.

My First Yoke

I have four siblings, two sisters from my mother and two brothers from my dad's side. However, I did not meet my two brothers while growing up or as an adult, until one important day. 'Sis' is bossy, and everybody knows it including her. At work, my bossy Sis is over the union, which suits her well because she gets to tell people what to do. She has told me what to do all of my life and felt the need to continue when I became an adult. My 'Other Sister' is a busy body who manages to find her way into everybody's business. Growing up with my sisters was great, and we had a good relationship with one another. However, there were a few times I had to say to Sis, "Come on now! I am grown, and I don't need you to tell me what to do." Apparently, she did not get the memo; so let's just say, that's when the problem came in that broke my relationship with Sis in half.

My Dad and I were very close. He was a very handsome, manly man, and I could trust him. When I was a child, I would run and jump into his arm. He would catch me and rub his facial hair on my face. I loved that! He taught

When You Fast

me how to fish, use tools, and the way a man should care for a woman. Throughout adulthood, my Dad was a handyman for my sisters and me. I could rely on him, and we remained close. To me, he was a very good father and I thank God for him.

Years later, Dad became ill and was in the hospital for a while. On one occasion, Dad asked me to contact his sons, because he wanted to see them. He sensed he would die soon. I talked to one of my brothers, and his reply to our father's request was very disturbing to me. My brother said, "He was no Dad to me." I replied, "If Dad passes do not come to the funeral." Well, my father did pass away. Sis took it upon herself to be in control of everything. I did not like her choices for Dad's funeral. I did not want my two brothers to come because I had never met them. However, Sis asked the criticizing brother to attend the funeral. I was upset! She knew how he felt about our father because I told her. She chose not to acknowledge my feelings and instead, asked me for some pictures of Dad. My reply to her was, "Pictures! I'm not going to do a picture show. Oh no, I don't want to do the pictures."

When I arrived at the funeral home on the day of Dad's funeral, Sis was trying to introduce me to my brothers. I could not believe it. Here I am sitting in the front row of my Dad's funeral pouting, heated, and tearful for so many reasons, and my two unknown brothers sat behind me. I was so "fired up," I wanted to set it off! Led by anger, for a moment I imagined myself jumping off the pew and diving on Sis, then just swinging my arms to land blows on her like a jackhammer busting concrete. With tears flowing down my cheeks, I managed to redirect my mind to Dad and got through the funeral service painfully quiet.

Now I thought Sis's actions handling Dad's arrangements were bad, but the next thing she did really pushed me over the edge. Sis asked my Other Sister to call me and share the plans for a private service to spread my

When You Fast

Dad's ashes. Sis chose to do it on his birthday, which was a month after his death. I told my Other Sister I was not emotionally ready to do that so soon, and to tell Sis to wait. Despite my request, Sis continued with her plans and invited our brothers too. Unwillingly, I went to the service. I asked my Other Sister to tell Sis I wanted some of my Dad's ashes. I felt like an outsider, because I didn't want to attend this service. When I discovered our brothers were there, I WAS ENRAGED! Really! Did Sis forget one of these brothers didn't want to be associated with Dad? This service was private and for those who 'loved' my Dad, yet there were the 'unknown' brothers. Now, I really was not going to talk to her for the rest of my life. I was done, done, done with it!

When I decided to shut Sis out of my life, I had forgotten about our mother. Mom had Alzheimer's; and as it progressed, she went to live with Sis in Lexington. Although my feelings about Sis had changed, I loved my Mom. I could not, and would not, let my feelings about Sis

Barbara Y. Tuggle

keep me from seeing my mother or helping to care for her any way I could. Sis took very good care of our Mom during the year and a half that she lived with her. She kept my Other Sister and me aware of everything going on with Mom. When we talked on the phone about Mom, it was brief. After a while, Mom became ill and was in and out of the hospital. Sis decided to bring Mom to Louisville to be closer to family members who could keep an eye on her. Mom was in a nursing home, and my sisters and I each had a day of the week to visit. I knew part of the responsibility to care for her was mine. Yet, each time I spoke to Sis about Mom's condition, I became angry. She had a way of pushing all my buttons. Although it was not Sis's visiting day, I could feel her presence when it was my turn. Even the staff at the nursing home seemed under her control, and I felt them negatively leaning on me. One of my male cousins reminded me that Sis was grieving the loss of our father too, and she was doing so in her own way. Yet, I still had a major

When You Fast

problem with her and did not understand that excessive controlling nature. By now, the yoke of bitterness and resentment I held towards her was heavier. Each time I heard Sis's voice, the weight of her burdensome control was unbearable.

After my Dad passed, I joined a new church and had to attend orientation. It was the hardest orientation I had ever done. There were five books to complete, and each book took five weeks of study time making the course 25 weeks long! Let's just say, I cried each time I went to class. While in class, I realized the bitterness in my heart was now hate for Sis. God spoke to me through scriptures, and each one became personal. For example, here is some of what I heard:

- Ephesians 4: 31-32, "Get rid of bitterness and be compassionate."

- John 10:14-15, "If you do not forgive Sis of her sins, I, Your Father will not forgive you."

Barbara Y. Tuggle

- Mark 11:25-26, "When you are praying and you remember that you are angry with another person about something, forgive that person. Forgive them so that your Father in heaven will also forgive your sins."

That last scripture did it for me. Immediately, Sis came to my mind, and I repeated the words, "So my Father in Heaven will not forgive my sins?" My heart was broken into pieces. I had been talking to my Aunt about my feelings towards Sis, and she said I could not hate anyone, especially my sister. I did not want to hate Sis, but as I said, she had a way of getting underneath my skin. However, I knew I had to do it, and so I forgave her.

Months later, a dear friend's boyfriend passed away. She was in love with him, and I felt her grief. As we were driving to his funeral service, my friend shared how she wanted the service to go one way and his family wanted it to go another way. Having no input in the arrangements for the love of her life hurt deeply and she felt left out. Naturally, I could relate since I had the same experience with Sis

When You Fast

controlling everything. I can imagine God saying, "It is time to set my daughter free," because that day while I was driving my friend to the funeral, God showed me I had not forgiven Sis.

For the entire trip, I was listening to my friend complain about what was going on, and then I snapped. The sun was shining in my car, and I could feel God close as if we were face to face and He said to me, "Listen to her. Does she sound like anybody you know?" I started crying as hard as I did when my Dad passed away. I pulled myself together enough to blurt out to my girlfriend while sniffing and snorting between words, "When you go into the church, do not say anything about your disappointment. Just go sit down and be quiet. You did not have the right to plan his funeral. You were not married. So, his mother can do what she wants to do."

The sun was shining even brighter, and I could feel the heat. Let me just say, I thought the heat was coming from the sun. Suddenly, I remembered what my cousin said about how Sis was grieving just like me. Then I heard God say to me, "You know My scripture, you know My Word. Now you are telling me you have forgiven Sis. You have been lying to yourself. You have my Word in class to show you what I need you to do for Me, and you been telling Me you have forgiven Sis." By this time, I was sobbing uncontrollably and forgot my friend was in the car, who by now probably thought I lost my mind. I began begging aloud, "God, forgive me. Forgive me. I'm sorry. I do forgive Sis. I do forgive my sister." Then I pulled my sniffling, whimpering self together, and told my friend I was sorry but this was between God and me. She got out of my car, and I could tell she was mad. God used the circumstances of my friend's grief to get through to me. God uses people, situations and anything to teach us what He needs us to understand. On that day, I received God's message loud and clear.

When You Fast

In a conversation with Uncle Charles, I told him about the incident that day and he said, "God knows what is inside of us, and He has a way of bringing it out." We began talking about breaking every yoke and he said, "You know, Sis is your yoke. She does not know where you are in your life now, and she is treating you as though you do not know God for yourself." At that point, I realized my problem was not with Sis, it was with my flesh. Just as Uncle Charles said, Sis was treating me like I did not know God for myself. I was acting as if I didn't know Him. The scripture in I John 4:20 sums up my yoked situation with Sis perfectly.

> "If we say we love God but hate any of our brothers or sisters in his family, we are liars. If we don't love someone we have seen, how can we love God? We have never even seen him. [21] God gave us this command: If we love God, we must also love each other as brothers and sisters. (ERV)

Let me just say I was living with this mess for close to a year. Sure, I said I loved God, and I do. I was doing all the 'right' things, so I thought. The one exception was my efforts to justify holding onto anger because Sis was bossy, and I thought she intentionally hurt me. While listening to the lies I told myself, the burden of my relationship with Sis became a heavy unbearable yoke. It was choking the life out of me and cutting off some awesome blessings. Make no mistake, God does not bless mess. Things changed when I emotionally broke down in the car and lashed out at my friend. Instead of being a blessing to my friend, I attacked her. My spirit was fighting my flesh and the Holy Spirit was Referee. I may have been a silly woman throughout that year as I hosted my own pity parties, but I came to my senses on that day. While down for the count, I knew I had to get it right! Today, I know forgiveness comes from my heart towards Sis and not just something I say; I truly mean it.

My Second Yoke

While writing this book, I was hyped up on the idea. I spent most of my time reading the Bible, praying,

When You Fast

researching and fasting. Everything was falling into place. I shared my progress with three girlfriends, and each one shared their newly discovered thrill of online dating sites. They told me of their fun meeting, talking and dating men from this site. At first, I thought that's great for them; because my mind was on finishing this book. As I talked with each of them from time to time, their adventures and excitement began to leave me feeling left out. After all, it had been four years since I dated and I never thought of being alone for the rest of my life. So I asked my daughter to sign me up too. She posted my picture and a brief bio, and later that evening I got a few hits. Well now, that's what I'm talking about. I've still got it! I proceeded to chat with a few of the guys online and accepted an invitation to meet one of them in a public place. Although our brief meeting did not lead to my wanting to see this man again, I was definitely hooked on the dating site and I was having fun too. A few more dates and a lot more chitchat and before I knew it, a few weeks had passed. In that time, I had not written anything nor was I studying and praying as much. Finally, I met 'Him' and we connected. After a few phone calls, we decided to meet face to face. He invited me to dinner at a restaurant near my home. We recognized each other from pictures posted on the dating site, greeted, and he leaned in for a momentary embrace. We went inside the restaurant, and I sat across from him. My mind was racing with thoughts of how fine he was; just pure eye candy with deep dimples, nice skin, and a tall, lean basketball frame. I call him Mister Remote Control because he definitely turned me on. He was a straightforward person, and I really liked that about him. We had great conversations before and after we met in person, and I felt very comfortable with him.

One evening Mister Remote Control invited me to his home. It was a nice house, but he did not have living room furniture. The living room was an office, so we went to his bedroom to watch television. We sat at the foot of the

When You Fast

bed, and then he moved real close to me. I could smell his cologne. It was intoxicating, and I kissed him and he kissed me back. His lips gently moved across my cheek, and he began to whisper in my ear. I listened to his voice, as the words seemed to find their way to different parts of my body and started a fire at each point. I had not felt that warm, tingly feeling in a very long time and it felt good. The caress of his hands tenderly moved over my body while pulling me closer. I was wilting in his arms and I said, "I needed to go," and he said, "I know," then he pulled me even tighter into his body. We were becoming one as both our bodies responded to each embrace. The passion was rising fast, and we just couldn't stop. His hands were all over me! I whispered, "I really need to go." He replied, "Yes you do." I was fading to black, when suddenly I heard in my head, "Get out of here!" I do not know how I jumped up from his embrace, but I did and ran to the kitchen to pull myself together. Mister Remote Control followed me. I turned and kissed him and quickly went out of the back door. I headed for my car while fumbling for my keys. After settling in my seat, I took a deep breath and said aloud, "God, what is that man doing to me?"

All the way home, I could feel something was wrong but I did not know what it was. I felt heavy and a little sad. Naturally, when I went to bed that night Mister Remote Control was on my mind and I was restless. At times, I replayed the evening as if it was a movie, but relieved that I did not have sex with him. I prayed for God to give me peace and the answer about how to handle my feelings. I knew that man was not for me, but that did not stop me from wanting him. When God sees I am ready for a man in my life, I will know it. The next morning, I deleted my profile from the dating site. I knew I had to put as much time into God and my book as I once did. In fact, now I needed to turn it up. So, I ignored his calls and text messages. Let me just say it was very difficult because he stayed on my mind. However,

When You Fast

when the devil is tempting us, God gives us signs and we have to pay attention. My involvement with Mister Remote Control brought out the old Barbara. In one of our conversations he said, "Only you can let people do what they do to you." He was right. I said and did things while with him that I thought I had control over, and I did during the four years without a man in my life. However, I discovered there were still things holding on to me after Mister Remote Control and I met. I remembered a particular verse in Isaiah 58 about the need to break every yoke. I was willing to let go and get back on track.

> "You need to do more in your everyday life. Fasting is just the beginning. You have things that have a hold on you. You need to break every yoke." **(Isaiah 58:3-5) ERV**

I Peter 5:8 tells us to: "Control yourselves and be careful. The devil is your enemy, and he goes around like a roaring lion looking for someone to attack and eat."

Barbara Y. Tuggle

Now we are clear on the meaning of a yoke and the things that keep us from experiencing God. You can take this opportunity to look at yourself by answering some serious questions. Are you in an unhealthy relationship? Do you struggle with alcohol or drug addictions? Are there various problems troubling your family and stressing you out? Is a career change in your future, but you are afraid to take that step? These things are yokes. Whatever you know is delaying you from living a satisfying life, write it down so you can fast for a breakthrough. Give the issues of your life to God and let Him show you how to handle them. As long as we carry yokes, we cannot see our blessings. The weight of anything that stops true worship and service to God spiritually weakens us and eventually breaks us. Therefore, the yoke must be broke.

How to Break a Yoke

First: Schedule Time to Fast

When You Fast

Make a decision to set aside time to fast and pray. We all have a major responsibility to get rid of anything affecting our relationship with God. However, we cannot do it without God. And so, we have to make ourselves available to hear from Him. Anytime we think we do not have the strength to get rid of a load, God can. We must be willing to give it up and patient enough to wait until He takes it off.

Second: Confess

In this section, there is a page where you have an opportunity to identify any yokes in your life. Confessing the yoke is a necessary step to becoming free. You do not have to announce your confession to someone—just tell God. This is your chance to acknowledge the burden and its effect on your life. Before you begin to write, take a few minutes to replay the events in your head that led to the yoke. After you gather all the facts, think about this: Is the yoke a person, place, or thing? When did you first feel it? Who is responsible for lifting the load of the yoke? And, this is big: What role do you play? Write everything.

Third: Ask Forgiveness and Forgive

Perhaps the act of forgiving is hard because it is not in our nature to be ready to admit we made a mistake—just plain wrong! Let's get real. Everybody wants to be right even when we know we are wrong. But look at it this way. You can't get 'all the way' free if you don't 'all the way' repent. That is why confessing our problems and messes to God are important as well as identifying the key players. It helps us to recognize who is at fault. A place or a thing cannot be at fault, but a person can. Therefore, if fear (which is a thing) is the problem, we need to ask God to show us where it is coming from and to forgive us for acting fearful. We know that the majority of the time, our unforgiveness points to a person. However, the way we handle ourselves in the situation determines whether we need to ask

When You Fast

forgiveness too or make a decision from our heart to forgive others

Fourth: Maintain the Victory

When we get rid of the burden, it does not mean we are weak or that we are giving in to the persecutor. What it does mean is that we take control over our flesh and do not allow anything or anyone to stop our blessings, especially a burden. However, we have an enemy (the devil) who once had us bound and does not want to see us walk in victory. Therefore, we have to guard and control ourselves.

If you are wondering 'What does this have to do with fasting?' Let me say it has everything to do with the success of your fast. Depriving yourself of food or a personal pleasure is not easy. It costs us a personal sacrifice each time we go on a fast, and we should expect something in return. Otherwise, what is the point? One outcome we should expect is to be able to stomp on struggles instead of bowing to burdens. We should expect to be a little wiser each time we come out of a fast. However, the most important expectation we should have when we fast is to hear God without a doubt. Fasting spiritually cleanses us if we are open to being clean. I do not believe I would have ever forgiven my sister had I not been fasting. Why? Because I would have shut God down by not listening to Him, then continue to run my own plan, which was to stay as far away from Sis as possible. Consequently, I would have stayed in bondage to bitterness and hatred as well as missed so many blessings. Today, I am free to love my sister and accept her as she is. As for Mister Remote Control, it was never about him. Instead, God showed me I had to be free from lustful desires. I also needed to see who was most important to me, was it a man or God. I am so thankful God has given us fasting as a spiritual tool to use as we go through life and deal with issues. However, it is an ongoing process to

When You Fast

maintain the victory, and God gave us equipment for that too. God will speak to you whether you fast or not. But if you want a clear understanding without distractions of your own personal influences—try fasting. It works!

Barbara Y. Tuggle

MY PERSONAL YOKE(S)

If you are wearing a yoke, get real about it so you can break free. List your yokes here--<u>all of them</u>. Yokes hurt so find scriptures to apply to the scars and wounds for healing.

When You Fast

THE FULL ARMOUR OF GOD

Once yokes have been broken, it is important to guard our heart to avoid becoming bound again. If we want to keep it real, everyone has an enemy somewhere. It could be someone you know. Some people in other countries hate the United States; therefore, all residents in our country are their enemy. However, spiritually speaking, everybody on earth has the same enemy. This enemy looks for weak people, those who no longer give attention to spiritual matters, and those who are going through rough times. That enemy has many names: the devil, adversary, evil one, Satan, the accuser, deceiver, or whatever. This enemy tempts us, so we can become failures. When we fast, all kinds of temptations hit us hard to weaken our minds, so we will not complete the fast nor hear from God. These temptations are strong and distracting and come from within us or people the adversary uses to influence evil with the intentions of killing, stealing and destroying us. I can only speak for myself. The devil used the love I had for my daughter as a distraction against me. Because she is my child, I know when she needs help or is hurting. I think every parent knows about his or her children. However, to keep my daughter from experiencing hurt and any discomfort, I always stepped in, gave in, or did what she asked. This caused a problem because I knew there were times I should have let her work things out. I gave in to that temptation to save her and stepped in anyway. Finally, I realized she was a grown woman with children, and I needed to let her try to work things out whether she could or not. Giving in to that temptation was robbing me of time and was emotionally draining. It was a hard pill to swallow to let her be herself and be independent. So you see, it is not always an evil thing tempting us, but it can still be a distraction. What things does the enemy use to tempt you? How can we stop the enemy?

We have another spiritual tool to help us whether we are fasting or not. It is the full armor of God. Every day we

When You Fast

can put it on for protection against evil. The description of the armor and directions for putting it on is in Ephesians 6:10-18 (NKJV). Read the scripture below and circle the six pieces of amour found in this scripture.

> "¹⁰ Finally, my brethren, be strong in the Lord and in the power of His might. ¹¹ Put on the whole armor of God, that you may be able to stand against the wiles of the devil. ¹² For we do not wrestle against flesh and blood, but against principalities, against powers, against the rulers of the darkness of this age, against spiritual *hosts* of wickedness in the heavenly *places.* ¹³ Therefore take up the whole armor of God, that you may be able to withstand in the evil day, and having done all, to stand."

> "¹⁴ Stand therefore, having girded your waist with truth, having put on the breastplate of righteousness, ¹⁵ and having shod your feet with the preparation of the gospel of peace; ¹⁶ above all, taking the shield of faith with which you will be able to quench all the fiery darts of the wicked one. ¹⁷ And take the helmet of salvation, and the sword of the Spirit, which is the word of God; ¹⁸ praying always with all prayer and supplication in the Spirit, being watchful to this end with all perseverance and supplication for all the saints"

Barbara Y. Tuggle

Time to Get Dressed

Let's talk about how the full armor applies to fasting. As soon as you plan to fast, the thought of not eating enters your mind negatively. If you set a date, you will want to change it. If you decide not to eat a certain food, suddenly you will see it and want it. If you plan to give up something like watching television, a new favorite program series begins when you plan to fast. Darn it! Keep in mind, all these things happen <u>before</u> fasting. What I am saying is, you are in a fight before you begin fasting. Think about what it will be like after you start. I don't know about you, but if I am in a fight I want something besides my fists to defend myself. Who goes to fight unprepared? Really! A weapon would work for me, especially if my fight is against someone stronger than I am. Armies prepare for combat, and boxers put on protection before any fighting. Real fighters get prepared mentally and physically. What can Christians do to prepare for a fight?

When You Fast

First, we need to know who we are fighting. Ephesians 6 says it not against people on earth. We are fighting against the rulers and authorities and the powers of this world's darkness. We are fighting against the spiritual powers of evil in the heavenly places. Then verse 13 tells us how to prepare for the fight when it says, *"That is why you need to take up God's full armor so you can fight against the devil's clever tricks."* We need to wear the full armor to fight, and we need it when we fast. Another thing about fighting against spiritual powers is to know the weapons the enemy uses. As I said earlier, distraction is a weapon used when we fast, and it is an attack on the mind. The enemy 'gets high' on our reaction to bad thoughts going through our mind. The devil will not give up and will tempt you all of your life, especially with sins of the flesh like jealousy, money, food and your personal desires. The closer you get to God, the stronger the devil will attack you. Every day we need to get dressed in our full armor and remind ourselves throughout the day that we are wearing it. There is a reason to wear each piece of armor, so let's take a look at how it works against our enemies.

The Armor Protects...

- *Helmet of Salvation* – Put it on your head to protect your spiritual mind. Give God your mind and your life, and believe Jesus died for your sins and rose again. Keep prayer in the forefront.
- *Breastplate of Righteousness* - Only the pure and holy can wear it, for they have the grace of God in their heart. Treat others the way you want to be treated. Be honest, good, humble, and fair. Live, as God wants us to live by having good relationships and obeying His commandments.
- *Belt of Truth* - Wear it to be true to yourself and the truth of God's word. Know God's word. Truth keeps us from being in the world, and we cannot love God and desire the things of the world more than we desire Him. The world has a different outlook on how we should live and what we desire as Christians.
- *Feet Shod with the Gospel of Peace* – Have peace with God, so you can walk in peace as you spread the gospel. Be content when times are hard.
- *Sword of the Spirit* – This is the Word of God. Study the Word because it has power

When You Fast

and changes your life. Trust that God will speak to you in His Word. The verses will come alive, so you will see His will for your life. Be able to speak the Word with your mouth and follow through with it by the way you live life.

- ❖ *Shield of Faith* – Faith is being sure God will keep His Word. Have faith when spreading the Word of God. Faith in God protects us when we are tempted or doubt anything. Without faith, we cannot please God. Hold your shield of faith out in front of you always.

Barbara Y. Tuggle

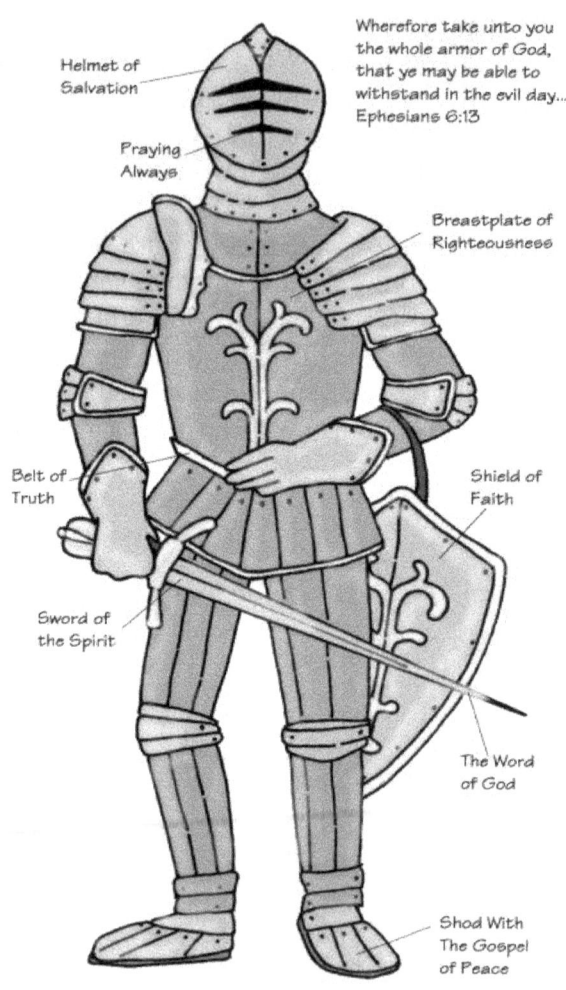

When You Fast

Now that you know what each piece of the full armor of God stands for, here is an exercise to do often. Physically stand up then go through the motions of putting your armor on and say aloud the purpose of each piece.

- Put your hands on your head and say, *"I put on the helmet of salvation to protect my mind and thoughts."*
- Smooth your hand over your chest down to your stomach and say, *"I put on the breastplate of righteousness to guard my heart."*
- Put both hands behind your back and bring them to the front (as if you are putting on a belt) and say, *"I put on the belt of truth knowing God's truth keeps me free."*
- Bend down and touch both your feet (sit if you must) and say, *"I put shoes of peace on my feet so wherever I walk I stand on the peace of God and I act peacefully."*
- Pick up your Bible, lift it high and say, *"This is the Word of God and it is alive in me. I speak, live, and trust God's Word as truth to take down my enemies."*

Barbara Y. Tuggle

❖ Finally, lift both your hands, close your eyes, and say, ***"God, you are my shield and my faith is in <u>You</u> to guide, protect, and keep me from temptation. I trust <u>You</u> with my life.***

It is a good practice to put on the full armor when you think a fight or a struggle of some kind may arise. For the most part, that could be every day. The important thing to remember is to start putting it on the minute you feel you are being tempted or attacked. Your words do not have to match those I have suggested, but what you say does have power. Soon, you will learn what each piece protects and it will become easier to say it aloud.

Make a copy of the picture in this book of the fully equipped soldier and post it where you will see it daily. Remember, fasting is a spiritual tool; and in order to be effective, you have to guard yourself against attacks by reading the Bible, praying, and wearing your full armor too. It works. I am a witness.

Part Three

LET'S DO IT!

When You Fast

WHAT TO EXPECT WHEN YOU FAST

I cannot sugar coat this for you, so I'll just say it. Fasting requires determination. It will sound like a reasonably good idea for whatever reason until you try it. Since I have been there and done it, here are things you can expect and ways to move on pass quitting. Even if you fast one day, it will be hard at first. Why? Because most of the things that are good for us are challenging, and we are tempted to quit as soon as it gets hard or seems harder. We have become a comfortable society in the United States, and we like 'easy' anything. Fasting is not easy, but it is the most rewarding thing you can ever do for yourself. As you continue fasting, I give you my word the sacrifice you make is worth it! So don't get *"scared"*—you got this.

Expect to Want Food

Everyone has an emotional connection to food. It starts from birth. Usually when a baby cries, one of the first things moms and dads think of is that it must be feeding time. A baby's cry does not necessarily mean the child is hungry. However, the association to food is still present for both the caregiver and the baby. Is it any wonder that many adults use food for comfort when they are sad, depressed, or heartbroken? In addition, some people use food to reward themselves when something great happens. This is another developing habit from childhood. In these examples, there is an emotional connection to eating. This type of connection is not a good thing because we give permission to our bodies to control our desire for food. The emotional connection to food does not go away when you are on a fast. In fact, it gets stronger; so, you have to **be prepared to fight it** and you will win.

One way to get ahead of this game is to prepare food in advance and keep a food journal. Another important way to fight the urge to eat is by eating foods that are filling and

When You Fast

nutritional. While fasting, write down everything you eat along with how you are feeling at the time. However, you must be completely honest and include all the details so you have a clear picture of what is happening. The good news about wanting food is, the more you fast the less you will hunger for food as your body becomes quiet then you can become hungry for God.

Expect to Fight Your Flesh

When you fast, you need self-control over your flesh. Talk out loud to yourself. You aren't crazy for doing that, and I am not crazy for telling you to do it. However, try not to draw attention to yourself in public because some people will not understand what you are doing. You can start by saying things like:

"Flesh you do not crave _____ *(fill in the blank with whatever it is tempting you)*. You will not have control over me. I will not live by being led by my flesh. I will fast today and it will not be a problem. I will do what I need to do to maintain a close personal relationship with God. I will seek God's will in my daily living. I will read the Bible. I will be kind and considerate. I will not please my flesh. I will show honor to God. I will help people in need. I will make this fast mean something to me. I will give up things that are not pleasing to God. Dear Lord, please help me with this fast. Give me the strength to be strong."

These statements will raise your spirits to be strong, and God will break your hunger for food. If you are fasting something other than food, this is still effective to fight against temptation.

When You Fast

Expect to Feel Left Out

Timing is everything when you choose to fast. It is not a good idea to fast when a special event is planned where high calorie foods will be served such as at, family reunions, holidays, birthdays or other celebrations. However, when God tells you to fast it could be anytime. So, expect to feel left out if you attend the function or excuse yourself if the challenge of going will be too great. Those who are new to fasting are more likely to feel 'left out;' however, it can happen to the best of us. As you include fasting in your lifestyle, resisting the urge to eat will not be as difficult. Now that also depends on how long you are fasting.

Here are some examples of how to excuse yourself from events including food service, so you won't have that uncomfortable 'left out feeling.' If you go to an event and happen to be having a rough time emotionally and/or physically, expect someone to ask why you are not eating. It is not necessary for you to tell the guest or host you are fasting. Simply say something like, "Everything looks great, and I am sure it tastes even better, but I don't care for anything now." Or, "No thank you, I'm good." Period! Then quickly change the subject or excuse yourself immediately and go to an area where people aren't eating. Do not continue the conversations with anyone who is inquiring, because he or she will not stop asking you until you answer to their satisfaction. If the event includes a sit-down meal, call the host, tell him/her you could stop by but you will not be dining, and leave after your short visit. And you could just excuse yourself by saying you have another engagement, then leave. Yes, you will have another engagement somewhere else—at home—where there are no tempting food choices. If you get an invitation to a game party, and you're fasting television, thank the host and tell him/her you have other plans and can't make it.

When You Fast

Fasting is not easy, but it is also not a burden. It is not necessary to cause stress for yourself by avoiding questions from guests or making different food choices just to stop feeling left out. You know what tolerance level you have, so just use wisdom. Also, do not let the devil beat you up because you decline an invitation while on a fast. It won't be the last time someone invites you anywhere. Remember the purpose of spiritual fasting is to get closer to God, and you can't do that while continuing your normal lifestyle when you fast.

Expect Some Physical Changes

Some people may not be able to fast food, but everyone can temporarily give up something like using the phone other than for emergencies or business, watching television or giving up certain shows like reality shows, soap operas and all types of sports programs or using your credit card for long periods. The important thing is to remember is to give up something that gives you the <u>most</u> pleasure or convenience. The physical reaction to fasting 'things,' is always going to be positive. You can expect to have a change in your attitude about whatever held your attention because it will no longer be as important as it was; especially the more you fast those 'things.' Fasting food should be limited to a set time because it can be harmful to our body if we go too long without eating. When fasting, most people will experience some physical reactions. These are not symptoms of fasting; it is the reaction of cleaning our bodies of years of poor eating or for overall cleansing even though you eat healthy food. Fasting stirs up toxins in our bodies as they begin to leave, and that can cause some discomfort. It doesn't last, and you feel so much better after you've fasted. Below are just a few of the common physical reactions to fasting food. However, these reactions may occur because of the type of fast you are doing and your specific body.

When You Fast

Everyone is different, and you can have a reaction that is not listed or you may not have a reaction at all.

- ❖ Bad breath—our lungs is an organ that waste passes through during the elimination process, and air also comes from our lungs which can cause bad breath. Brush your tongue and rinse with mouthwash to solve the problem. You can also chew on some mint to freshen breath and of course chew gum.
- ❖ Tiredness—Especially on a water-only fast; so get to bed early. The extra sleep will be good for you.
- ❖ Diarrhea—Fruits and fruit juices can affect everyone differently.

Remember these reactions are your body's way of telling you it does not like the shake up, but there are things you can do to calm your body. As you continue fasting, you won't notice the reactions, because you will know what to expect and what to do to press through them.

Barbara Y. Tuggle

Expect To Learn Some Things about the Real You

Sometimes getting to know who you really are is more uncomfortable than those reactions I just talked about earlier. Let's just say the picture you get may not be pretty, but it is necessary if we want to be a better person and I do. Since you are reading this book, I think you want to be a "better you" too.

We started this journey with my introduction, and I told you I was going to be real with you. I've shared some personal stuff. Now I'm really going to let you know some deeper things about ME. I found out I was a hot mess! I am not proud of what I learned about myself, but I am grateful that I know now because knowing was the beginning of changes in my life. One of the things I asked God to do during my fasting times was this:

When You Fast

"God show me the real me. I want to free myself up to focus on You."

I got what I asked for with this one and like I said, it wasn't pretty but it was necessary. I realized that I was a rude woman. For instance, I am always in a hurry when I go to the grocery store. When I arrive, I quickly grab a cart and speed walk down the aisles. Sometimes I would ride up close to the back of a person pushing their cart to make them go faster or move out of my way. Yeah, I was one of those people who would zoom pass you so fast you could feel a breeze. I never went as far as having 'grocery store road rage' but when I said, "Excuse me," my tone did not sound very polite. The person I was talking to would turn and look at me; they saw my body language displaying impatience as I said under my breath, "Really!" Oh, and I have been known to roll my eyes a few times when I got irritated with everybody in MY way. I showed no patience.

Barbara Y. Tuggle

During one of my fasting days, I had 30 minutes to shop and I needed to be out of the grocery quickly to go to physical therapy. I tried to rush people to make my schedule work. As I was zooming from aisle to aisle, I kept running across an older lady shopping. It appeared that every aisle I turned down, she was there. At one point, she turned and looked at me. Instantly, I saw every person: male, female, older or younger that I had actually bullied into moving out of my way when I shopped. That scared me, so I turned my cart and went down the next aisle slowing my pace. I picked up a can good to read the label and saw my hand trembling and my body began to do the same. At that very point, I realized I was rude. When I saw the many people a few moments earlier, God was showing me that not only had I been rude to this woman but also I have been rude in other areas of my life. Tears flooded my eyes. Immediately, I began to repent and begged God to forgive me. I felt so ashamed of my behavior, and I asked Him to show me how

When You Fast

I could make it better. After pulling myself together, I went to check out. There I was standing in the cashier's line behind two other older women. One of them did not know the pin number of her debit card to pay for her food. The other woman apparently brought her friend to the grocery and was getting impatient as her friend continued to try the pin number. The older woman said, "I just can't remember the number." The other woman replied with more irritation in her voice, "I don't know when I will be able to bring you back to the grocery store." I felt sorry for the older lady and thought to myself, "Oh my God, thank You for giving me this opportunity." I told the older lady not to worry about it. I would pay for her groceries and to write down her pin. I had no idea how much her bill was—it didn't matter. I saw God giving me a chance to be a blessing. The older lady thanked me and both women left the store.

The cashier said I was a Godsend and I replied, "No I'm not, I am just in a hurry." Although the cashier saw a kind Barbara, the real me had another motive. MY thought was, 'If I pay for her groceries, I can move on. But I also was thanking God for giving me another opportunity to do the right thing by someone who was on the receiving end of rudeness.' I could clearly see what rude behavior looks and sounds like. The thought of my acts of rudeness in any way to someone else made me so grateful to see 'me,' and immediately I stopped. Those two women were a Godsend to me, and I received a very valuable lesson that day in the grocery store.

That's not all. I realized I was selfish. I work at a children's hospital—the largest one in the state of Kentucky. It is a beautiful place to work located in downtown Louisville. I transport patients to various parts of the hospital and it can be a busy place, which often seems to make the time fly on the night shift. I love my job. I have worked on my job for 14 years and never established any close relationships with my co-workers. I went to work, did

When You Fast

my job and stayed out of their conversations and personal business. A simple "hi and bye" added to "let's have a good night" was as far as my exchanges went. It wasn't that I didn't like them; I just chose to keep my distance. I didn't need them to help me do my job. Each day I walked in the door, I was confident that I could handle mine. That is until something unexpected happened to me, and my 'I got this' attitude became as low as a balloon that has lost air.

On one of my scheduled weekends off, I was in a car accident. If you have ever had an accident of any kind where your body took a blow or two, you know that soon after you begin to feel the aches and pains. The night of the accident was okay at best until the wee hours of the morning somewhere around 3 a.m., I could not feel my legs and that numb feeling moved up my body to my waist. It was very scary for me to take a step and not feel anything. Days later, I still suffered from this numbness. Was this numbness temporary or leading to some type of paralysis? I thought.

Barbara Y. Tuggle

My work schedule would resume on Monday night, but I was still numb that morning. My frightful, nervous thoughts were, 'How am I going to push stretches if we have a busy night? I have to work, but how can I?' My hope was that my coworkers would help me push the stretchers and wheelchairs to get me through my shifts until I was back to normal, but we did not have a relationship. I thought I needed to 'soften them up' so they would want to help me do my job, so I decided to make a treat to take to work. Since I was on a fast, flavored popcorn and infused celery-mint-cucumber water would be perfect, and I can eat it with them. While making the popcorn, I began to think about my coworkers and my thoughts turned into selfish ones like, 'What have they ever done for me?'' or 'It's not like they help me with my work' and 'They make more money than I do, and I did not like to give to people who already had something.' I got to work a little earlier to set things up. That night, rather than being very busy, I had no wheel chairs

When You Fast

or stretchers to handle and there was no need to ask my coworkers for help.

For the first time in 14 years, I made an effort to communicate more with my coworkers as we all shared my treat. I was more relaxed with them and got to know them better, and they were able to do the same with me. Having an easy night was great. I read and talked, but most of all, I heard God and saw Him work things out for me despite my plan to soften my coworkers. I had not trusted God to take care of me, and staying in my world all those years was so selfish. I did not see my coworkers as a benefit to me or my job, and more importantly, I was not a blessing to them. How could I pray for them or for anything going on in their lives, if I did not spend the time to have a relationship with them as friends? I could not let my selfish attitude cut off my blessings or theirs. I had to get that right! Once again, I asked God to forgive me.

Barbara Y. Tuggle

During a follow up with my doctor, she told me of her concern about my legs and ordered an MRI as soon as possible. At first, I was scared, and then I realize how ungrateful I had been to God. Before the accident, each morning I would say thank you for waking me up and that all my limbs are moving. But let's just say it was a different type of "Thank you God" and not totally honest. It was more out of routine. The thought of my routine morning "Thank you" made me feel ashamed. Now at a moment when I was facing the possibility of something scary happening with my legs and back, I wanted that "Thank you" to mean more and have more power. I do not ever want to treat God as if He is 'a routine' like brushing my teeth in the morning. When we come close or do actually lose something that we take for granted will always be there, our "thank you" is more sincere but it should be that sincere all the time. We should be especially sincere about our gratefulness when there is no threat. I know I am now. Again, I asked forgiveness.

When You Fast

Rude, selfish and ungrateful...hmmm...that was the old messy me uncovered, so I could be free. Those were all uncomfortable revelations I received throughout different fasting times. God loves us enough to correct us, and He loves us enough to encourage us too. God confirms that He cares, sees everything and will show/tell us things we are doing right also. God showed me: I love a challenge, I like praying for people, I am humble, direct, have a big heart, and I love deeply and I am loved deeply by Him. I am a work in progress like all of us. I know God is not finished with me. The process of purging me from the inside out is something I want and will always cooperate with God in order to be who He wants me to be. I am so thankful that God has mercy on me and does not reveal all my mess at one time. Regardless of how uncomfortable it is to find out areas in my life that need to change, I am stronger from knowing what it is, and I will remain on guard so I won't continue to act that way.

Barbara Y. Tuggle

Expect to Hear God's Directions

Since I began to fast, I have heard directions from God more clearly than I ever have in my life! God told us he would give us a Comforter, the Holy Spirit, who would also guide us. I work third shift and one morning about 5 a.m., things were slow, so I was reading one of my books on fasting. Suddenly, the Holy Spirit told me to write down the word 'breakthrough.' I did not want to do it. I had a bad attitude this particular morning and it would not be long before I would be going home, so I did not write it down. The word came up again, so I gave in and wrote it down. I kept on reading my book, and a little while later the Holy Spirit said to write down the word 'powerful.' I said okay, but look I was getting mad. Time seemed to pass slowly, and then the Holy Spirit said to write the words: 'temptations, sacrifice, believe,' and 'victories.' I was so tired, and I wanted to go home. For some reason, this whole

When You Fast

thing was a struggle for me. When I got finished writing the words, I looked up and said, "What am I supposed to do with these words." The Holy Spirit said in a gentle voice, "Write your testimony." I snatched my paper and wrote my testimony. I cried because I felt conviction pouring over me. I did not want to take the time to write now and I wanted to go home. But the more I wrote, I felt God's compassion. Here is my testimony.

I will give my <u>testimony</u>. When I get my <u>breakthrough</u>, I need to <u>sacrifice</u> all my old beliefs and be with <u>believers</u> before I go on my <u>fast</u>. It will be powerful and uplifting. I will have the <u>victory</u>.

When the Holy Spirit tells you to do something, you need to do it without hesitation. I could have missed my blessing through rebellion. The Holy Spirt continued to give me the following words: 'distracted<u>, circumstances, power,</u>

Barbara Y. Tuggle

honored, rewards, temptations, glorify, wisdom, trust, intimate, hunger, blessings, obey, great worth, He told, let go, who are,' and I wrote into a testimony as directed.

I will honor your name every day. I will not let my circumstances overpower me by the temptations that were in my life. The rewards I seek when I fast will glorify me. I will not get distracted; I will do what I need to do for you.

I will trust in the Lord with all my heart. I will not let my circumstances ruin my blessing. I am going to let my wisdom show me how to be intimate with the Lord. I have a hunger in me that will not let me stop seeking Him.

I will obey God and find out what my great worth is. He told me to let go of my old ways. Who are you to tell me I cannot do it? I will show you all.

When You Fast

Each of us is important to God. He wants to talk to us all the time, whether we are fasting or not. It could be one word at a time or many. He knows which words fit everybody. When you fast, it has to be done with the expectation that something great is going to happen for you. Expect to hear from God when you are busy 'doing you,' as well as when you are praying directly to Him. When you fast, listen and write your testimony with the word or words you receive. Ask God to lead you and explain to you anything you hear and may not understand. Trust me when I say, "He is waiting and expecting you."

When You Fast

LEADING BY EXAMPLE

It would be crazy for me to write a book about something I have never done. As I explained earlier, I have fasted the wrong way and now I fast the right way. At this point, I can show you better than I can tell you. So, before moving on to the next few pages, I'm going to get you started using portions of my journal entries from different fasts. These examples can help you in preparing for your first fast. There are blank forms at the back of this book for you to use when you're ready to start. The first box on the next page is for you to check off what we have talked about so far. If you do not have a complete understanding of these seven points, I suggest you go back and read that particular section again.

Barbara Y. Tuggle

FASTING CHECK LIST *Put a mark in the Yes/No column to verify you know the fasting process.*		
	YES	NO
1. Do you know what a Christian fast is?	✗	
2. Do you know what to expect when you are on your fast?	✗	
3. Do you know how to get your testimony?	✗	
4. Do you know about the different types of fast?	✗	
5. Have you identified any yokes?	✗	
6. Have you read Isaiah 58:1-14 and understand what God needs you to do while on a fast?	✗	
7. Have you signed your covenant to complete a fast?	✗	

The next sections are about planning for the food you will eat, and foods you want to eliminate. For me, it was important to list the foods I loved to eat. As you see from what I wrote, most of these foods have a lot of calories, fat and not much nutrition. But, they make us feel good while we're eating them. I am not suggesting we never eat these dishes ever. But in order to discipline myself for this particular fast, I could not eat some of these foods. So I drew a line through those items on the list. If I were to fast a thing

When You Fast

instead of food, I would list that in the second box entitled:

WHAT ARE YOU GIVING UP ON THE FAST? (Food or Something Else.)

WHAT FOODS DO YOU <u>LOVE</u> TO EAT?	
List some of your favorite foods in the columns below	
Macaroni and cheese	Cold cereal
Hamburgers	Fish
~~Pizza~~	~~Bacon~~
~~Stuffing~~	Cheese
~~Sweet bakery goods~~	Bread and butter

WHAT ARE YOU GIVING UP ON THE FAST?	
(Food or Something Else)	
Pork	Food with additives
Junk food	Sugar or added sugar

WHAT FOODS WILL YOU EAT ON THE FAST?	
Rice	½ cup of orange juice/day
Nuts	Fruit
Different vegetables	2 slices of bread a day
8 ounces of chicken divided into small portions to last one wk.	Cheese

When You Fast

Next, I start laying out my plan that focuses on expectations during the fast, plus my Bible study and praying times.

MY FASTING PLAN – 7 Days			
Date to start the fast	March 15	Date to end the fast	March 20
How are you feeling now about starting this fast?		I am excited. Need to change my attitude about a few things.	
What do you want to accomplish during this fast?		God show me the real me. I want to free myself up to focus on you.	
When do you plan to study the Bible?		Study the Bible while I am at work	
What time(s) will you pray? *(A time different from normal prayer time)*		I will pray while I am at work, in my car and, when I visit my mother.	

Barbara Y. Tuggle

MY FASTING PLAN – _7 Days_			
Date to start the fast	March 15	Date to end the fast	March 20
What or who will you pray for during your fast?		I am praying that I do not have to have back surgery	
What bad habit do you need to change?		Stop being judgmental	
What is one of your long-term goals?		Have classes to teach about fasting. Have retreats & camp for kids & go to prisons to teach about fasting.	
What is one of your short-term goals?		Complete my book by a certain date. I want to do some volunteer work.	
What did you learn during this fast?		God showed me some personality traits that I need to work on	

REMEMBER: Keeping a daily personal journal during the fast, helps you stay on track.

When You Fast

Since I work third shift, I eat breakfast at different times, for instance, 12:00 p.m. or 4:00 p.m. Following are several more examples of my fasting periods. Here you see: the foods I gave up, what I ate, what I expected from the fast, my activities, and some outcomes. I still complete pages that record when I will start and finish.

Barbara Y. Tuggle

What I am giving up on this fast
I won't eat cheese, sugar, dairy, processed foods, meat, <u>no orange juice</u>! My water is pineapple, oranges, blueberries, and grapes. No television. No phone 6 a.m.- 6 p.m

What I will eat
Whole grain rice with pecans and raisins, fresh fruit, vegetables, banana nut cereal, and water infused with fruit

What I would like to accomplish on this fast
1. Write one or two pages for the book
2. Learn how to be with myself
3. Say something positive to everyone.
4. Some type of volunteer work or help somebody in need.
5. Help my daughter with my grandbabies, pray for my uncle, pray for my pastor, and others
6. Help my daughter move—Teach my grandbabies about God
7. Have a better relationship with Sis
8. God I'm not asking for a man, I ask you to get me ready for the husband You have for me
9. God to show me who I am

Activities I will do while on this fast
Go hiking with my grandbabies and host scripture parties

When You Fast

I don't always give up meat during a fast. One of the foods I found to be the main dish for me when I am fasting is kale greens with turkey polish sausage. I start a fast and end the fast by eating this as a meal because it really helps my digestive system. Another biggie for me is giving up sugar. Remember, pecan pie is one of my favorite deserts. I never knew there was sugar in just about every type of food we eat, except meat. When I fast sugar, it really limits what I can eat. We need to look for sugar on the labels of food. Manufacturers hide sugar in food by using different names for sugar like: agave nectar, blackstrap molasses, cane sugar, glucose solids, confectioners' sugar (powdered sugar), galactose, maltodextrin, and diastase. All of these are processed sugars and are in foods that you would not have thought about unless you read the label. Canned vegetables contain additives as well, so make sure to eat fresh vegetables. If eating frozen vegetables, again read the packaging label.

Dairy is a food product that I enjoy, especially butter. When I cook, I put butter in just about everything. On one of my fast, I chose not to eat dairy. Two days before the fast, I cooked rice and added butter and cheese. While at work, I pulled out my lunch dish and put it in the microwave. It smelled *soooo* good. OH NO! I realized it was the butter and cheese I added and remembered I was not eating dairy. I made a mistake and did not have food to eat for lunch because I did not want to cheat on my fast. I learned a lesson from that one, which is to write down what I cannot eat and keep it where I can see it.

As you can see from my notes, the fast I was on doesn't have a large selection of foods. By this time, I had been through a few fasting periods and it was not hard for me to downsize my food intake. In fact, it had gotten easier. When I fast, one fast is usually different from the last. Some

When You Fast

fasting periods may also vary from hours to days or weeks and include food or I may only fast 'things' and eat normally. I eat a lot of rice when I fast and it is filling, especially, when combined with meat, fruits or vegetables which makes it tastier. Stock your cabinets with lots of spices, raisins, herbs and a variety of nuts—if you are <u>not</u> allergic to them to enhance the flavor of food. Beans are another good food to help you feel full. We all have our likes and dislikes when it comes to food. Some people don't need a lot of seasoning, while others do. If you are fasting food, whatever you eat is not going to taste like 'mom's home cooking or a holiday meal feast.' It's a fast! And you CAN be satisfied and full without feeling like you are punishing yourself. I have become very creative as I continue to fast. I've learned to change the way I prepare food, added different kinds of foods to my grocery list, and created my own new recipes. Food prep has become part of my planning process in getting ready to fast and it keeps my mind busy. Some of the food combinations I've tried were never repeated because it just didn't work for me. I repeat other dishes each time I fast. Invest in a few cookbooks written for vegans or specifically for fasting. Most of us have a least one cookbook at home, or you can borrow one and copy recipes to change and fit your taste buds while fasting.

Managing Your Time

When you begin to fast, I recommend you fast from dawn to dust. If you cannot fast during that time, ask God to show you when to begin. For myself, I now fast for two or three weeks at a time. Because of the discipline I have gained through fasting, I have learned to fill up my day with things that do not center around food whether I am on a fast or not.

We all can get used to something when we have to, and that goes for eating something else instead of what we want. Or doing something else instead of what we want to

When You Fast

do. We talked about emotional eating earlier in the section that often leads to eating. Often when we are not active or become bored, eating comes to mind. If I have a rough day or a lot of free time, one thing that works for me is taking my mind off eating by listening to instrumental music. I may need to take a walk or do something that I have not done in a long time. The point is for me to relax and not stress about what I can't eat. As my mind settles, then I pick up my Bible and let God into my world.

Earlier I shared that I was in a car accident. Well while writing this book, I was actually involved in four car accidents. All of them could have been worse. My car was banged up and so was my back, but my spirit was good about what happened. My doctor told me I would need to have surgery on my back in order to feel better. Really? I was not trying to hear that, and I was scared to schedule surgery. I began physical therapy and I was feeling better, so I tried

Barbara Y. Tuggle

to continue my active lifestyle, especially hiking with my grandbabies. That was our thing! I would push through the pain and often suffered later. Some days were better than others were, but I was determined to live my life in spite of how I felt. This was a tough time for me because I was not fully able to enjoy my personal physical activities or those hikes with my grandbabies the way I wanted. During this period, I continued to fast and realized it was more important for me to schedule my time with activities that were not as physically challenging especially while I was recuperating from the accidents.

One night while at work during my lunch break, I remember something Brother C told me in our conversation. He said, "We all have 24 four hours in a day. What are you doing with your 24 hours?" I had been reading one of my books about fasting and it said, *"...as soon as we get through eating, we look at the clock to see when we can eat our next meal."* I had finished my lunch and had the very same

When You Fast

thought before reading that sentence. Then I came up with the idea of using a picture of a clock to show me what I was doing with the 24 hours in my day. I wanted to know how much time in my day went to praying, reading the Bible, time with family and friends, watching television and more. Time can get away from us. Don't you agree? Where we think we have spent it wisely, we soon find out we wasted a lot of our time on things that didn't promote growth or serve a real purpose. I certainly found that out when I filled in the time around my clock. I thought I was praying more than I was, and I was surprised at the amount of television I watched. Using the paper copy of the clock helped me see that I should plan something productive for each hour on the clock. Scheduling certain times for Bible study and prayer, represents how I account for time spent on things that are in my best interest. It makes me value each minute, so I can try to use my time wisely. I advise you to try it. 'Time accountability' is not something I suggest doing every day, but I include it in my life every so often to help keep me on track. Now, I am an 'old school' woman knows technology is not my friend. Things change faster than I can keep up with, so I use the face of a clock to record my time. However, for some of you with stronger technological ability, using your iPhone or Android phone is more effective. You can schedule time on the calendar, set alarms for reminders, and view your day. The best part is that you can conveniently set the activity to repeat for any given length of time. I can do some of that on my iPhone, but I also like my paper copy. In case you want to use the clock, I have inserted a blank one in the back of this book. I hope you try it at least once.

When You Fast

Preparing for Fasting

Several years ago, I cleaned houses part-time for extra money. Since I had a full-time job, I could not have too many homes to clean but I needed enough to make it worth my time and fit my schedule. I had to plan when I could work, how much time it would take to clean a house and the amount I would charge. To make this all work, I had to prepare before I began to clean the first house. I took an inventory of the cleaning supplies and equipment that I had and then made a list of what I needed to buy. Next, I gathered my supplies and equipment, then store most of the items in the trunk of my car, which would save time for me when moving from one job to the next. During that time, with careful planning and a few adjustments, I was able to earn the extra money I needed and handle a routine that did not interfere with my full-time job, family, or social life.

Barbara Y. Tuggle

I approach fasting the same way by using careful planning. Through my research, I discovered recipes that I could prepare in bulk so I would not have to think about what I was going to eat when it was time for a meal. If hunger has caught up with me during a fast, let me just say when it is mealtime, I am ready. I don't want to do anything, but heat the food up and eat. Learning something is one thing, putting it into practice is another. Consequently, I have also learned a few lessons the hard way, but now menu planning is part of my routine. Since fasting is part of my lifestyle, I stock certain food items usually eaten during a fast. So when I take an inventory, my grocery bill is not so high. In order to be successful at fasting, we have to plan for it before we begin it. I usually need two days to prepare for a fast. This includes planning activities, what I want to accomplish, cleaning my refrigerator, grocery shopping and cooking food I will eat during the fast. Making a list of foods you love to eat, but plan to give up is easy to do on paper. It takes

When You Fast

determination to list some foods when you know your desire is to compromise. So be true to yourself. Remember, part of fasting is sacrificing your pleasures.

A Little Bit about Nutrition

If you have **never fasted, I advise you to get medical and spiritual counseling** before you start. My nutritionist holds a license in the state of Kentucky and is a Clinical Nutritionist, MED RD, LD. I asked her for the number one piece of advice about eating healthy. Her response was, eat food grown from the ground not in a factory. Don't eat too much processed food from boxes, bags or cans which often contain preservatives and artificial flavorings. These are foods to avoid as much as possible. The nutritionist told me to eat four meals a day and stay around 1500 calories a day. I was not surprised when she said I eat too many sweets and too much bread; I love both of them. After analyzing my food labels, she gave me substitutions for what I need to eat. With the exception of eating too many sweets and bread, I would bet most people should follow the advice of my nutritionist.

Robert Tidwell is a friend who has been working in the food manufacturing industry for years. For as long as I've known Robert, he has been very conscientious about the contents of food regarding additives, processing and its effect on our bodies. He always researches food products. He and I were discussing fasting, and he gave me a greater appreciation for reading labels. This guy has changed the entire way he buys food and eats. Robert is healthier and more energetic now than before watching what he ate. Here is his insight on nutrition.

"Understanding what you eat and the effect that it has on your body is just as important as how much you eat. There are many chemicals added to our processed foods than are not good for us. Some of us don't know or care what is in our food. If you are one of the people who does

When You Fast

*care, it is very easy to find out the contents of products thanks to improved labeling. The USDA and FDA say that every food item has to have a list of all ingredients on the package. Doing a little simple research will give you a much better understanding of what is going into your body or help you decide if you want to eat the product at all. I chose to research an ingredient; trisodium phosphate (**TSP**), which is in one of the boxes of breakfast cereal I like. TSPs is an inorganic chemical used as a cleaning agent, lubricant, food additive, stain remover, and degreaser. Now I don't know about you, but I don't want the same chemical used in 'stain remover' in my breakfast cereal. The ingredient label is your number one tool for understanding what is in the food we eat and the affect it has on us. If you see an ingredient on the food-packaging label you don't recognize, simply look it up. It only takes a few minutes, but the information is priceless in your quest for better nutritional health. It is our*

Barbara Y. Tuggle

responsibility to know what we are consuming and the affect it has on our bodies."

The additives Robert is talking about that are ingredients in our food, adds to a number of toxins in our bodies that we take in from other external toxins as well. Make no mistake; it is impossible to avoid all of the toxins that come with living our life; for example in the air, water, various home and personal products, drugs and tobacco. But, we have the power to control how much we take in, and we can do something to get rid of as much of it as possible.

Since my appointment with the nutritionist and talking with Robert, I make it a point to read the labels and include their advice in my eating habits whether I am fasting or not. Each visit to the grocery store reveals more. Honestly, I am shocked at the amount and kinds of chemicals that are in some of my favorite foods. I had no idea! Food I use to eat, I no longer eat. Now I love reading labels and

When You Fast

this 'research girl' looks up the meaning of those additives and chemicals regularly.

Increase Water Intake

Drinking at least 6-8 glasses of water every day is probably one of the hardest things for people to do. Most of us don't realize the true importance of drinking enough water every day and the affect it has on our health. We drink lots of liquids, but most of what we consume is not pure water. Although there is more water in sweet tea and lemonade, it is not the same as drinking 100% water. Remember those toxins my friend talked about earlier, water helps flush them from our body if we drink enough. Think about how much water we consume if we drink 8 ounces of water as follows:

- One glass in the morning when we get up
- One glass before breakfast

Barbara Y. Tuggle

- One glass with a morning snack
- One glass before lunch or with our meal
- One glass with an afternoon snack
- One glass before dinner (while preparing your meal)
- One glass with dinner
- One glass about 2 hours before bedtime

At the end of the day, we will have drank eight glasses of water in a day, which is 64 ounces. Wouldn't that be great! You can expect to use the restroom more than usual because all that water will come out, but it will be worth getting rid of waste. One way to help get the water in our bodies daily is to infuse our water with natural flavor. Water doesn't have to taste boring. Make it refreshing. Infusing your water with natural fruit or vegetables or herbs flavors can make it much easier to reach your daily goal. I have had fun experimenting

When You Fast

with different flavors, and one of my favorites is water infused with cucumber, celery, and mint.

While fasting, I advise you to stop drinking anything with caffeine in it such as coffee, tea, and soft drinks. These types of liquids can speed up or slow down your energy level. You will see better results if they are not part of your liquid intake. Consequently, start cutting back on them about a week or two before you start fasting. This will make it easier to move into the fasting routine with caffeine during your fast.

There are times when I choose to fast and other times when God tells me to fast. When everything is good and I am happy, I go on a praise fast to thank God for the goodness He has already shown me in my life. During this kind of fast, I am not expecting God to give to me; instead, I am giving God attention and love. He is worth it! Other times, I know I need to fast and this is how. I feel like I have nowhere to go…nowhere to turn. I feel like everybody is

Barbara Y. Tuggle

living his or her life and they are happy. I tell a few close friends or family my problem and it seems like it is no big deal to them, and then I feel even worse than I did before the talk. So I tell someone else and they just don't understand. Then I cry out for the Lord to hear my cry and that's when I know it is time to fast, so I can get in agreement with God. He knows what is going on in our lives, and He gives us different ideas about our situation other than what we thought about. I don't think I am alone here. Can you identify with anything I just shared? If so, it is time for a fast.

When You Fast

IT'S YOUR TURN TO FAST

Before beginning to fast, make an appointment to talk with a nutritionist. If you prefer, your doctor can answer the following questions, and maybe without making an appointment. All doctors have medical assistants who will give questions to the doctor, and call you with his/her response. If it has been a while since you visited a doctor, an appointment may be necessary. As for your meeting with a nutritionist, this will need to be a face-to-face appointment. Below are questions to ask either professional:

1. Ask if there is any particular food you have to eat when taking medication that must be taken with food
2. Ask what fast is best for you when you fast—tell them what you plan to do
3. Ask if there are any limits to how long you can be on a fast

4. Ask how much food you need to intake normally for your health on a daily basis

Next, find someone who will be in your corner—a spiritual advisor or close friend who understands what you are about to do. I cannot say this enough; I've got your back! If you need help, need to talk or have additional questions, please email me at whenyoufast@gmail.com. I am excited for you, and I applaud you for taking this step.

You are ready so let's do it! If this is your first fast, start with one day or two and work your way up to more days. If you remain steadfast, soon you will be fasting for a week then one day you will go much longer. Fasting should be limited to a specific predetermined length of time. Nobody knows your body like you do, so plan a fast that suits you. You can always challenge yourself to go longer as you continue the fasting process without causing harm. If fasting is not new to you, ask God what food you need to give up. When there's something heavy going on in your

When You Fast

life, completing a one-day fast may not be enough. You may need to fast several days or a week or more. Or, you may need to get close to Him by not watching television, no cellphones, no contact with friends, no husband, and no grandbabies—I hope you understand what I mean. Just spend some alone time with God. It is important that you understand this is a spiritual adventure between you and God. The following pages contain some 'check lists' to prepare you for your first and future fasting times, like the ones I showed you in the last section. Take time to think about each question on these lists before you answer because your responses will be like a roadmap for you while on the journey. This is part of the planning process.

Getting Ready for Your Fast

1. Pray for guidance to get a start date and the type of fast you will complete

2. Make a decision to take personal responsibility for your fast

3. Plan activities for yourself while you are fasting

4. Plan to spend time with believers

5. Plan time to study the Bible and pray

6. You need a testimony, so make sure you have a journal to record details of your fast

7. Make a grocery list of foods you need to purchase in preparation for the fast

8. If you do not like tap water, purchase bottled water

When You Fast

The next few pages are planning guides that I showed you in the section entitled **LEADING BY EXAMPLE**. These pages are blank, so you can begin to fill in your responses and finalize your fasting plan. If you need help, refer to that section. Included at the end of the book are more blank guides that you can copy as you plan for more fasting times. As you continue fasting, you will find that it will not be necessary to use all the guides.

Journaling

Before I started fasting, I did not journal and I never kept a diary as I was growing up. However, now it is an indispensable tool for me. It is so rewarding to go back and read my thoughts as I continue through the fast especially when I go for longer periods. Although some people just don't like writing, please don't let that stop you. It is not important to write each sentence perfectly. Remember you are not writing for anyone else. Your journal will contain your thoughts, views, joys, and pains. It is very important to write down as much as you can during the journey and especially when God speaks to you. With the technology we have on hand today, recording your journey is at your fingertips using your iPhone/Android phone, tablet or computer. It really does not matter what form of journaling you use, as long as you try it and be completely honest with yourself.

Here are a few things to write in your journal to get you started:

- ❖ What are some signs that show the fast is working for you?
- ❖ Have you seen a change in your life?
- ❖ Did God reveal something to you?
- ❖ What will you do about the thing(s) that has a pull on you?
- ❖ Have you broken your yoke?

When You Fast

- ❖ How do you feel about praying and reading scriptures during your fast?
- ❖ How has your attitude changed when you fast?
- ❖ Can you see yourself making lifestyle changes?
- ❖ Has God called you out of your comfort zone?

If you cannot answer any of these questions, do not be discouraged. Maybe you need to go on a longer fast to allow time to experience a change, or maybe after you go through more fasting times you are able to have a response. The purpose of these questions is to get you started with journaling. You may have a different way of recording your experience. I hope you find what works for you as a reference point for future fasting times. It is such a blessing to go back and read the prayers God has answered, directions

Barbara Y. Tuggle

He is giving, and your impressions of what is going on. If you keep up with journaling, you will see growth in your spirit, attitude, and the way you look at things. Please don't miss the opportunity to experience this.

Now grab your favorite pen and start planning your fast.

When You Fast

FASTING CHECK LIST

Put a check in the Yes/No column to verify you understand the fasting process.

	YES	NO
Do you know what a Christian fast is?		
Do you know what to expect when you are on your fast?		
Do you know how to get your testimony?		
Do you know about the different types of fast?		
Have you identified any yokes?		
Have you read Isaiah 58:1-14 and understand what God needs you to do while on a fast?		
Have you signed your commitment to complete a fast?		

Barbara Y. Tuggle

Before beginning your fast, you should have all **YES** boxes checked. If **NO** is checked in any boxes, go to the sections that discuss the topic and read it again.

When You Fast

WHAT FOODS DO YOU LOVE TO EAT?

List some of your favorite foods in the columns below

What foods will you eat when you are on your fast? Draw a line through the foods you will <u>not</u> eat.

Barbara Y. Tuggle

WHAT FOODS WILL YOU EAT WHILE ON THIS FAST?

When You Fast

MY GROCERY LIST

Foods I Have	Need to BUY

Barbara Y. Tuggle

WHILE YOU ARE FASTING

Start Date:		End Date:	
How are you feeling now about starting this fast?			
What do you want to accomplish during this fast?			
When do you plan to study the Bible?			
What pleasures are you going to give up?			
What time(s) will you pray? *(Pick a time different from normal prayer time—if possible.)*			

When You Fast

What activities will you do to keep busy? *(Do not include work--pick fun things to do with other Christians or focus on completing goals.)*	

Keep a record of your each fast. This helps you stay on track.

Barbara Y. Tuggle

WHILE YOU ARE FASTING

What or who will you pray for during your fast?	
What bad habit do you need to change? *(Confess it/them out loud daily)*	
What is a long-term goal?	
What is a short-term goal?	
What did you learn during this fast?	

Keep a record of your each fast. This helps you stay on track.

When You Fast

BREAKING THE FAST

Okay, here is the last piece of honesty I will share with you. I was very proud of myself for completing my first fast without cheating. YES! For seven days, I maintained discipline. It was a BIG deal to me! But, those last few hours were tough. I was counting down the minutes, and planning what I was going to eat as soon as it was one minute past the final hour. Of course, it was going to be something I had not eaten for days, and I could hardly wait! I was just hungry for something other than fruits, berries, and vegetables. One minute past my final hour, I jumped in my car and drove to the nearest White Castle™. Since I do not want to assume that everyone knows what White Castle™ is, I'll tell you. It is an American regional hamburger chain that has been around since 1921, that is famous for its small, square grilled hamburgers. Sometimes people refer to them as 'sliders,' because cooks fry the burgers on a large greasy grill. But, I did not want a hamburger; I ordered one sausage, egg, and cheese sandwich. Well, it was greasy and small too, and I practically swallowed it. I bit into my sandwich while driving away, and finished it off with a few sips of an ice cold Sprite. ™

I can't begin to tell you how good that sandwich was—hmmm—and I enjoyed the three *(if that many)* bites I took. As I continued to sip on the Sprite during my 15-minute drive home, I was satisfied—at least for now. About 10 minutes after I had eaten, my stomach began to rumble like a volcano and a sudden urge to relieve myself was overtaking me. It seemed as though the last few blocks to my home were so far away, as my body began to signal me that I had better drive a little faster if I intended to make it to the bathroom in time. Finally, I arrived home and ran to the bathroom where the upchucking began. It was just an ugly scene, yaw. Now if you are sitting there laughing, that's all right too. Be glad about my warning, so the same thing doesn't happen to you. The truth is, my digestive tract had

When You Fast

been at rest while I was fasting. It did not have to produce much hydrochloric acid and pancreatic enzymes to digest what I had eaten. I did not know any of that when I first began fasting, because as I said—I always cheated. Breaking a fast is as important as preparing for a fast. Eating greasy foods is a definite no-no. And if you eat too fast, expect an eruption that will lead to a miserable outcome.

Remember this when you break a fast.

- ❖ Take it slow and eat small portions
- ❖ Chew your food well
- ❖ Eat solid foods gradually and wait 15 minutes to see if you are still hungry
- ❖ Do not over eat—you can always go back for another *small* serving
- ❖ Give your digestive system a chance to work receive heavier food again

Barbara Y. Tuggle

It took a few days for your body to adjust to fasting when you started. Now that you have stopped, it will take a few days for your body to accept the foods you have not eaten for a while. Give yourself that time. Since learning my lesson about breaking a fast the hard way, now when I come off a fast, I use a saucer as my serving size. And I incorporate all that I've told you.

When You Fast

Part Four

FEED SOMEONE ELSE

When You Fast

TRAIN UP THE CHILD

Having my daughter is one of the best things that ever happened to me, and she is my rock. I am very proud of her, and I know she is a gift from God. Her daughters are also 'my heart;' and at the time of this writing, my grandbabies were 9 and 11 years old. I know I will have to break myself from calling them "grandbabies" as they get older; but until then, I intend to hang on to that unless they make me stop. We all spend a lot of time together, and I have great memories. When I pick my grandbabies up from school, we have an opportunity to talk. If I am fasting, I don't allow electronics or radio playing in the car; only talking among the three of us. Most children are very sharp as they watch every move we make and ask questions about things they do not understand. My grandbabies know when I am fasting. No radio music or electronics game playing is one clue; but other times when asked if I am on a fast, they are usually right. During one fasting period, I gave up using lights in my home; which also included television. I put tape over the switches to keep me from switching them on because of habit. I gave up lights during that fast because it is something I use every day. I knew each time I reached out to turn on a light, it would remind me to pray. My grandbabies wanted to switch on the lights, even though I told them I wasn't using them. I did not tell them I wanted to increase my prayer time. When they went home, one of my granddaughters told my daughter I did not pay my electric bill because the lights were out. Of course, my daughter called me and I had a good laugh, but she did not think it was funny.

Spiritual fasting changed my life, and it is very important for me to continue teaching my grandkids about it. I try to incorporate them into my fast by sharing something about God each time we are together. Since they are young, I decided to begin with one of the most important parts of fasting to me; which is praying and reading the

When You Fast

Bible. I began teaching them how to pray for what they want, what they need and pray for people who do not believe in God. I knew my grandbabies needed to learn the Lord's Prayer found in Matthew 6:9-13. Nyla; my 11-year-old granddaughter, learned it quickly and could recite the prayer with no problem. Ariana was struggling, although she could read it well. Like me, she has to study a little longer to memorize anything. I did not know why it was so important for Nyla and Ariana to learn the Lord's Prayer. In my heart, I just knew they both had to get it, so I made a game out of it to help Ariana. I told her to say a little bit of it, and then I would say a little bit and so on. I prayed that someday she would recite it as Nyla had.

My mother passed away in August of 2016. She was a wonderful person and a blessing to my two sisters and me. We loved her so very much. It was difficult letting go of my mother, especially since I still had a tender heart from when my father passed the previous year. As I stood at my

Barbara Y. Tuggle

mother's gravesite, it was as though I woke up from a nightmare only to discover not having her in my life anymore was not a dream. I wanted to escape the reality of that scene. While my mind said 'run,' my legs would not move. I looked at my sisters and daughter and saw no way to exit. Then I looked over at my grandbabies; Nyla and Ariana, and heard them reciting the Lord's Prayer. They both got it! I was so proud of them. A gush of tears streamed down my cheeks, my body began to relax, and the stress of it all left. I just knew God gave me that piece of joy at a time I needed it the most. He gave me such a beautiful memory of my granddaughters, instead of a sad goodbye. It was as if God was saying, "Thank you, Barbara, for teaching my daughters about Me." His timing in answering my prayer for the girls and putting all the pieces together was perfect. Hearing them took the sting away, so I could let go and not run. I cannot thank God enough for my grandbabies, and we will always have the Lord's Prayer as our special time.

When You Fast

The special relationship I have with my granddaughters is greater than what I could have ever imagined, and I treasure each moment together. In addition to our playtime, both girls read scriptures to me. It is important for parents and grandparents to leave an inheritance of wisdom to their children and their children's children. My grandbabies were excited when I told them about writing this book on fasting, so my gift to them is sharing a part of what God told me to do. I asked my granddaughters to pick a scripture about fasting, write about it and then I would make sure it goes in my book. So they both took their paper, pens and Bible to a separate part of my home and the following is what they wrote.

Barbara Y. Tuggle

> **1 Kings 17:8-15 (ERV) -** ⁸ Then the LORD said to Elijah, ⁹ "Go to Zarephath in Sidon and stay there. There is a widow there that I commanded to take care of you." ¹⁰ So Elijah went to Zarephath. He went to the town gate and saw a woman there gathering wood for a fire. She was a widow. Elijah said to her, "Would you bring me a small cup of water to drink?" ¹¹ As she was going to get the water, Elijah said, "Bring me a piece of bread too, please." ¹² The woman answered, "I promise you, before the LORD your God, that I have nothing but a handful of flour in a jar and a little bit of olive oil in a jug. I came here to gather a few pieces of wood for a fire to cook our last meal. My son and I will eat it and then die from hunger." ¹³ Elijah said to the woman, "Don't worry. Go home and cook your food as you said. But first make a small piece of bread from the flour that you have and bring it to me. Then cook some for yourself and your son. ¹⁴ The LORD, the God of Israel, says, 'That jar of flour will never be empty and the jug will always have oil in it. This will continue until the day the LORD sends rain to the land.'" ¹⁵ So the woman went home and did what Elijah told her to do. And Elijah, the woman, and her son had enough food for a long time.

Fasting to me is when you get closer to God. You can't do anything that pleasures you. You can't eat certain things. You can't do something that makes you happy because then you won't have a lot of time for God. It is like Elijah in 1 Kings 17:8-15. He had nothing but God. God told him to go to a widow and she would provide for him. You have to make your life during and after your fast like both of their experiences. You have to care for the people with nothing and give up your extras in life. Elijah had nothing so the widow shared with him. The widow had only a bit of flour and a bit of oil. Since she shared, the widow would never run out of flour and oil until it rains in the desert.

--Sincerely Ariana – Age 10

To my Grandma-ma, The whole family supports you through your journey of writing this book.

When You Fast

> Ezra 8:23— "So we fasted and earnestly prayed that our God would take care of us, and he heard our prayer."

Fasting is an experience to get closer to God. It is something that you are supposed to do every so often so that you remember that nobody is more important to you than God is. Fasting is something that God had made so that you don't forget that God has made you, your father, your mother, your sons, your daughters, your brothers, and your sisters so you will learn and never forget that God is our Lord and Savior. Fasting is the sacrifice that you have to make in order to stay close to God. Fasting is like Ezra praying and fasting as he said, **"So we fasted and earnestly prayed that our God would take care of us, and he heard our prayer."** Ezra 8:23. Fasting is something that God has made. So when you break a fast you shouldn't just go immediately out because then you wouldn't have learned anything from that experience. You have to go out of it slowly so that you stay close to God. Then after breaking your fast you have to eat healthier and cut some of the extra things out of your life so that you still have more time for God, more time than you had for Him before you started your fast.

Sincerely Nyla — Age 11
Some people don't like you, and I don't either. I love you. I hope your book is successful.

Barbara Y. Tuggle

Wow—what a surprise! Those words came out of the hearts of MY grandbabies, and I could not be more proud of them! They laid a little wisdom on us with those scriptures. Ariana saw that God told Elijah to do something, and he did it. She also understood that the widow trusted Elijah as a messenger from God, and she did what he told her to do. Ariana got that both Elijah and the widow thought they had nothing; but all the while, they both had God. When WE think we have nothing, we too should get close to God through fasting. Trust Him and who He sends to give you more than enough.

Nyla always keeps it real. *I am still trying to get her to tell me who doesn't like me.* Anyway, her view of fasting deals with the importance of changing our life and staying close to God. She is right; fasting is a sacrifice we make. No one should come out of a fast and resume a life with the same habits, bad attitude or things we did that were not pleasing to God before beginning to fast. I agree with Nyla,

When You Fast

everybody should learn something from the fast even if it is just one thing. That is the importance of being hearing and being close to God.

We teach our children how to tie their shoes, ride a bike, good manners and to treat others the way we want to be treated. Those and other things are very important for preparing our children for life. However, fasting, prayer, and studying the Bible to establish a relationship with God, which is very important and that makes all those other things we teach our children a lot easier for them to learn. When you fast, I encourage you to train your children too.

Barbara Y. Tuggle

FEED MY SHEEP

[10] Feel sorry for hungry people and give them food. Help those who are troubled and satisfy their needs. Then your light will shine in the darkness. You will be like the bright sunshine at noon. **Isaiah 58:10 (ERV)**

Whoever is in your life; whether family, friends, neighbors, and coworkers, please do not wait to make sure things are right between you and them. Keep your relationships open, so you can share with them what you know about God. We all have heard someone say, "Tomorrow is not promised to us." When you fast and begin to experience even some small changes in your life as I have shared with you, share with somebody else how your life has changed through fasting.

I work a third shift job in downtown Louisville, Kentucky, in a beautiful building inside with gorgeous shrubs, colorful flowers and well-cared grounds all around the area. We, like other cities, have homeless people

When You Fast

sleeping at night right on the benches throughout the downtown area. One morning a few years ago when I got off work, I proceeded to take my usual route to I-65 leading to my home. While waiting for the stoplight to change at the corner of 1st and Broadway, I looked over to this huge circular, concrete landscape bench where I saw someone sleeping. The torn, dirty blanket wrapped from head to toe formed a cocoon around the apparently homeless person, and his or her personal belongings were nearby in a pile. The person did not move as the day began with the noise of increasing traffic and clicking from the shoes of people passing by continued all around. A few more guys stood near the bench appearing displaced while watching their surroundings. I remember thinking to myself, "The police need to get them. They are a disgrace to our city." When I returned to work the next evening, there were no homeless people around. They moved because they were hungry. Homeless people overcome their fears to find food and shelter. Think about it. Don't you think it takes courage to stand on a busy corner with a sign that tells others you are hungry, or walk up to someone and ask for money, rummage inside a trashcan or try to hold your head up while being judged by others because of how you look or smell? I know I would have to be desperately hungry to do that! Homeless people focus on where food is and how to get it because food is necessary for life. They move out of their comfort zone to get food, regardless of what is going on around them or what others think.

Hunger is a blessing because it makes us move. I was desperately hungry and didn't know it. Yes, I admit, I might have less patience than a crying baby wanting to be fed, but let's just say I was 'hungry' for a change when I talked to my uncle about the family reunion. Little did I know Uncle Charles' solution meant I had to let go of my pride, step out of my comfort zone and get hungry for God in order to deal with the stress and yokes in my life. When I

When You Fast

think back, it really wasn't about a family reunion issue. God set me up! He set me up for an overall change inside me! Although I did not know much about fasting, I did know God would answer prayer. And, if the only way I could get what I needed was through fasting, I had to move despite my past failures or what someone thought of me.

I can honestly tell you that while I was spending time with God during fasting; after some time I was convicted, and drastically changed the way I felt about homeless people. I don't know when it happened; but one morning, I looked at the homeless group on the corner and really saw them with great compassion and instead of judging. I wanted to help. I began regularly volunteering at the Salvation Army.

This is one of the many ways fasting changed my life! What about you? What are YOU hungry for? God will feed you spiritually, physically, and financially; then through Him, you can feed others. He that thirsts after righteousness <u>will be fed</u>!

"Blessed are those who **hunger and thirst** for righteousness, for they shall be satisfied." Matt. 5:6 (NIV)

It has been a pleasure taking you on this journey of fasting with me. I hope you have gained a better understanding of the process and won't let another day go by without planning and beginning to fast. I am so excited for you! Please let me know how you are doing *When You Fast!*

I will continue giving people my testimony about fasting, I pray you will join me and give your testimony too.

When You Fast

Final Thoughts

When You Fast

THINK ABOUT IT!

When we began the journey in Part One, I asked you to write what you expect to learn about fasting. Now that you have finished the book, take a moment to write down what you have gotten from the information I have given you. Then go back to the page where you made that entry and compare your notes. You will be pleasantly surprised.

Barbara Y. Tuggle

It's up to us to build a spiritual foundation to withstand the storms of life and stay on the path God has laid out for us. God knows we may stray from the path. But no matter how far we go, He's always there waiting to guide us back. The next pages are several scriptures that help me maintain a strong spiritual foundation and keep me on my path. My sincere hope is that you will read these scriptures when you are fasting. As you study your Bible, began to gather some favorites that speak to your heart as well. You will grow closer to God than you have ever been. I earnestly pray that you will see and feel the changes in your own life even more than I have in my life.

Be blessed, my friend!

When You Fast

SCRIPTURE REFERENCES

James – The entire book! It encourages us to endure and live bold Christian lives. It is about everyday living that reveals a faith that changes lives. It contains detailed information on challenges we face on a daily bases and how to handle them. You gotta read this!

1 Peter 1:3-25 – A call to Holy living and hope
1 Peter 4:7-11 – Be good managers of God's gifts

1 John 1:8 & 9 – God's forgiveness of our sins
1 John 2:1-6 – Jesus is our helper

Ephesians 1:1-6 – Spiritual blessings in Christ
Ephesians 2:1-10 – From death to life
Ephesians 3:14-21 – The love of Christ
Ephesians 4:1-32 – Unity of the body and the way we should live

Isaiah 54:17 – Weapons

Jeremiah 17:5-8 – Trusting in people and trusting in God

Psalms 34:1-22 – Praise
Psalms 142:1-7 – A prayer of David

Ezra 8:21 – A reason to fast

Hebrews 10:24 & 25 – Strengthen each other
Hebrews 11:1-3 – Faith
Hebrews 13:1-6 – Worship that pleases God

Matthew 5:1-12 – Jesus teaches the people

Barbara Y. Tuggle

Matthew 6:1-18 – What you do in secret
Matthew 6:25 – Put God's kingdom first
Matthew 7:1-28 – Be care about criticizing others
Matthew 6:16-18 – Jesus teaches about fasting
Matthew 18:15-20 – When someone hurts you

Mark 12:28-34 – Which command is most important

Luke 4:1-13 – Jesus is tempted by the devil
Luke 5:34 – Jesus the bride groom
Luke 37:41 – Be careful about criticizing others

Joel 2:12-14 – The Lord tells the people to change
Joel 2:28-32 – God will give His Spirit to all people

2 Chronicles – 7:14 - Marriage

Romans 7:14-25 – The war inside us
Romans 8:1-17 – Life in the spirit
Romans 12:1-20 – Give your lives to God

2 Corinthians 1:11 – Paul gives thanks to God
2 Corinthians 6:14-18 – 7:1 – We are God's temple

James 1:1-8 – Faith and wisdom
James 1:12-18 – Temptation does not come from God
James 4:1-10 – Give yourself to God

Deuteronomy 28:25 – Defeating your enemy

1 Thessalonians 4:1-12 – A life that pleases God
1 Thessalonians 5:12-25 – Final instructions and greetings

Galatians 5:16-26 – The spirit and human nature
Galatians 6:1-10 – Help each other

When You Fast

Planning Your Fast

Copy the following pages to use during your future fasting times.

When You Fast

FASTING CHECK LIST

Put a check in the Yes/No column to verify you understand the fasting process.

	YES	NO
Do you know what a Christian fast is?		
Do you know what to expect when you are on your fast?		
Do you know how to get your testimony?		
Do you know about the different types of fast?		
Have you identified any yokes?		
Have you read Isaiah 58:1-14 and understand what God needs you to do while on a fast?		
Have you signed your commitment to complete a fast?		

Barbara Y. Tuggle

Before beginning your fast, you should have all **YES** boxes checked. If **NO** is checked in any boxes, go to the sections that discuss the topic and read it again.

When You Fast

WHAT FOODS DO YOU LOVE TO EAT?

List some of your favorite foods in the columns below

What foods will you eat when you are on your fast? Draw a line through the foods you will <u>not</u> eat. Do not

Barbara Y. Tuggle

include foods containing additives or processed sugar on your list.

When You Fast

WHAT FOODS WILL YOU EAT WHILE ON THIS FAST?

Barbara Y. Tuggle

When You Fast

GROCERY LIST

Foods I Have	Need to BUY

Barbara Y. Tuggle

When You Fast

WHILE YOU ARE FASTING

Keep a record of each fast. This helps you stay on track.

Start Date:		End Date:	
How are you feeling now about starting this fast?			
What do you want to accomplish during this fast?			
When do you plan to study the Bible?			
What pleasures are you going to give up?			

Barbara Y. Tuggle

What activities will you do to keep busy? *(Do not include work--pick fun things to do with other Christians or focus on completing goals.)*	
What time(s) will you pray? *(Pick a time different from normal prayer time—if possible.)*	

When You Fast

WHILE YOU ARE FASTING

Keep a record of each fast. This helps you stay on track.

What or who will you pray for during your fast?	
What bad habit do you need to change? *(Confess it/them out loud daily)*	
What is a long-term goal?	
What is a short-term goal?	
What did you learn during this fast?	

Barbara Y. Tuggle

Write your morning and afternoon activities inside the rectangular box. Then use a different color pen to record your evening and night activities underneath the box.

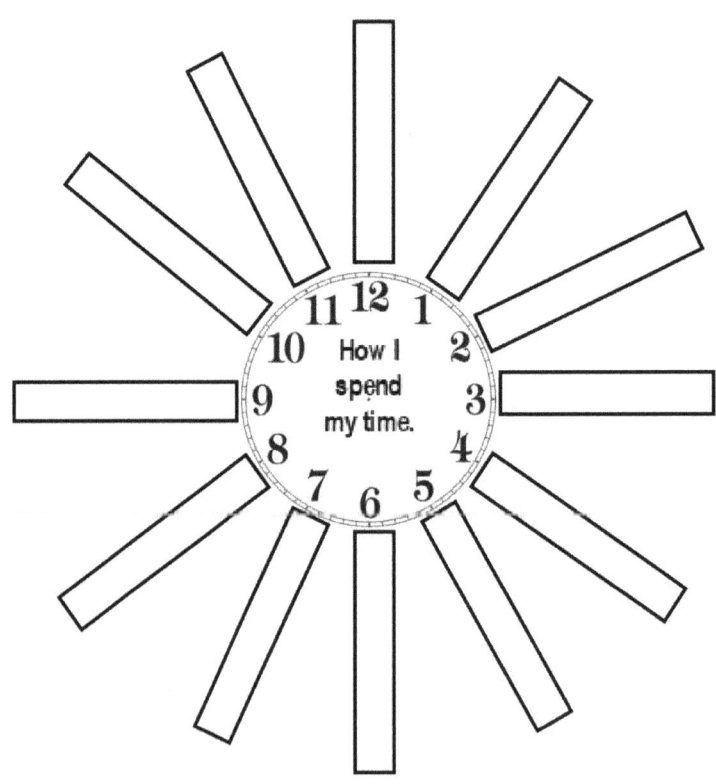

www.ingramcontent.com/pod-product-compliance
Lightning Source LLC
Chambersburg PA
CBHW071156160426
43196CB00011B/2103